IT'S ONLY THE HIMALAYAS

S. BEDFORD
IT'S ONLY
THE HIMALAYAS

AND OTHER TALES OF MISCALCULATION
FROM AN OVERCONFIDENT BACKPACKER

BRINDLE
& GLASS

Brindle & Glass
An imprint of TouchWood Editions
103-1075 Pendergast Street
Victoria, BC V8V 4E4
brindleandglass.com

Edited by Colin Thomas
Cover design by Margaret Hanson
Text design by Pete Kohut

LIBRARY AND ARCHIVES CANADA CATALOGUING IN PUBLICATION
Bedford, S., author
It's only the Himalayas and other tales of miscalculation
from an overconfident backpacker / S. Bedford.

Issued in print and electronic formats.
ISBN 978-1-927366-47-9

1. Bedford, S.—Travel—Anecdotes. 2. Voyages around the world—
Anecdotes. 3. Backpacking—Anecdotes. I. Title.

G465.B43 2016 910.4'1 C2015-907640-4

We acknowledge the financial support of the Government of Canada through the Canada
Book Fund and the Canada Council for the Arts, and of the province of British Columbia
through the British Columbia Arts Council and the Book Publishing Tax Credit.

Canada

The interior pages of this book have been printed on 100% post-consumer
recycled paper, processed chlorine free, and printed with vegetable-based inks.

Printed in Canada at Friesens

16 17 18 19 20   5 4 3 2 1

For Sara

PROLOGUE
Check, Please!

My mother: *Wherever you go, whatever you do, just . . . don't do anything stupid.*

I T WAS SUMMERTIME in Toronto. For residents who spent most of the year cursing the masochistic pioneers that'd selected this frozen landsicle (and not some coconut-strewn beach like their clever Spaniard counterparts) to be the New World, this was a cause for celebration. Parks flourished with life as dogs and lusty young couples frolicked under the shade of leafy maples. Patios were crammed elbow to elbow, pint to pint, as friends gathered in droves while exasperated waitresses crowd surfed with pitchers and hot wings. Canadians never let a drop of sunshine go to waste.

I, however, was miserable. And I had no idea why. All right, that isn't entirely true. I'd just dropped out of university for the second time. I was one of those crowd-surfing waitresses. I lived with my parents, which had its perks—such as no rent and the occasional happenstance of cut-up fruit in a bowl—but it also meant that, well, I lived with my parents. I'd thought that your twenties were supposed to be the ideal balance between the freedom of adulthood and the boldness of adolescence. It was the decade when the dreamers became the doers, when opportunity and full heads of hair abounded, and when potential was harnessed into tangible success.

And here I was, fucking it up.

Admittedly, it hadn't all been a wash. In between my attempts at academia, I had backpacked through Europe and Australia. In Italy, I tripped over the same cobblestones as the Romans one millennium earlier. And in Queensland, I was chased by a crocodile. Okay, okay, it was actually a wallaby—but not when I retold the story to my friends. In these moments, life was exhilarating and dirty and absurd, and I was ass-over-teacup in love with it. But then I returned home and became just another disenchanted youth with a drink tray, stinking of spilled beer and squandered vitality.

Worse still was that my friends were now all graduating, fresh-faced and full of earning potential. Some of them were getting business cards, for Christ's sake. Like Sara: she had always been intelligent, pragmatic, and successful in everything she pursued. While the rest of us flip-flopped over our majors like, ah, flip-flops, she'd flourished as a top nursing student.

After graduation, she also backpacked through Europe— although her experience was quite different than mine. My lackadaisical organization meant that, instead of following a sensible loop around the continent like most people, my route looked more like a map of the London Underground. Sara, however, had planned out every hour of her trip. Before she left, she even secured a position as an RN at a busy downtown Toronto hospital. I figured that when she returned, she'd move into a gentrified walk-up decorated with vintage furniture and potted herbs, and begin a happy life as a real person—while I'd continue to dither in pre-adult limbo.

But then she rang me up one August afternoon—her plane having just landed that morning—and my preconceived notions suddenly went sideways.

"It was the most incredible experience ever!" she gushed, high on life and jet-lag pills. "And not just the historical and cultural elements. I mean, that was great—to see in person what I'd learned about in school—but what I really enjoyed was the experience of travel. Obviously it wasn't perfect, because nothing ever is, but . . . that was the beauty of it. It was the challenges that made it an adventure and not just a vacation."

As she went on, I leaned against the windowsill and stared out at the world. The shadows were lengthening as the sky turned the electric blue found only at summer's end. I could see the moon already, a waning ghost trapped in the branches of a dead tree like a lost kite. Hearing Sara rave about her trip brought a bittersweet ache to my chest as I recalled my own adventures in Amsterdam and Edinburgh.

"I don't even want to unpack," she said, sighing. "I just want to go again!"

"But you must be stoked about beginning your life here," I countered. "You've got your career to look forward to, and you'll find an apartment soon."

"I'm not as thrilled as you'd think, Sue. After that trip, it seems like no matter what I do in Toronto, it won't compare." She paused. "Before I left I had this idea in my mind that I was going to do Europe, check it off the list, and then come back and commit to whatever it is everybody expects me to do here. But now, I don't think I'm ready to give up on traveling. In fact, I feel like I'm just getting started."

It shocked me to hear her talking like this. If I didn't know any better, I'd swear Little Miss Status Quo had developed some sort of wanderlust.

"I have a distant cousin who did a yearlong trip around the world when she was our age," I said. "It took her at least that long to save and prepare, but . . . god, could you imagine how awesome that would be? A year of excitement and ridiculousness and grit."

Sara groaned enviously. "Of escaping maturity and expectations."

"Of realization and self-discovery."

"Of just once choosing the fun path instead of the responsible path."

"Of no longer submitting to crappy jobs and haunting failures and cut-up fruit in a bowl!"

"What's wrong with cut-up fruit in a bowl?"

"Uh . . . never mind." We fell silent, each lost in our own radical sabbatical fantasy. A trip like that would be not only wickedly awesome, but also wholly transforming. And wasn't that the real reason why people traveled—to find themselves and answer such plaguing questions as *what the hell now?* To return with both a sense of direction and a stellar photo collection? It wouldn't quite be CV-worthy of course, but it *would* be a stepping-stone toward . . . whatever it was that the road inspired us to do.

"You know that if you ever were serious about something like that, I'd totally be on board, right?" I said. "Just say the word, and it's done."

"The word."

I laughed. "Sara, that's cruel."

"I'm not kidding. Let's do it. Why not?"

"Well, because . . . because . . ." I stopped. "Are you sure? I mean, it's not a big deal for me to abandon my pile of dirt, but don't you, like, have *stuff* to do?"

"Stuff can wait." I somehow heard her wave dismissively. "Why, are you telling me you *don't* actually want to go?"

I hesitated. Of course I *wanted* to go. After all, the notion of skipping through buzzy metropolises and hammocking on equatorial islands and searching for the five mystical Sankara Stones like Indiana Jones in *The Temple of Doom* (or whatever it was people did on such trips) would tempt anyone but the most diehard homebody. Nevertheless, I shook my head. "Uh-uh. No way."

"Why on earth not?"

Because what if I *didn't* find myself? What if, after seeing the sights and snapping the photos and reading the Wikipedia articles too late to fully appreciate what I'd experienced, I returned home the same as when I left—only with less money in my pockets and more sand in my shoes? Would I dust off my drink tray and become a chicken wing slinger once again? Would

I marry a potbellied bartender with the same name as my dad and raise the next generation of disenchanted underachievers? Then I wouldn't even have my blossom-scented daydreams to comfort me. I wiped my suddenly sweating palms on my jeans and swallowed hard.

Sara seemed to read my panicked thoughts "Have you ever thought about where your life is going?" she asked delicately.

"Never," I lied.

"Look, there's nothing wrong with being a waitress if that's what'll make you happy. But I don't think it will. And the longer you wait to make a move, the more comfortable you'll become, and the more afraid you'll be of change. You could get stuck here forever."

Forever, I imagined the disentranced underachievers whispering, and shuddered.

"The reason they call this kind of thing 'the chance of a lifetime' is because you only get *one*," she continued. "If you don't take it when it comes along, then you really can't complain about whatever happens afterward—or doesn't happen."

"Okayokayokay—you've convinced me!" This time I really meant it. "Just say the word, and it's done."

She laughed. "I knew if I threatened your right to complain, you'd agree to come along! All right then: The Word." *In the beginning, there was The Word*, I thought with a grin. *And the word was go.*

WE SPENT THE next year and a half saving and planning. The first day we gathered in Sara's bedroom—squealing gleefully and spilling tea all over the guidebooks—we decided to make a list of everywhere we wanted to go.

"Let's start with South America," I said. "I've always wanted to go to the Amazon."

"If we're going to do South, why not begin with Central?" Sara suggested. "I've heard great things about Belize."

"Okay. So we'll work our way down from Mexico to . . . uh . . . what's the one at the bottom?"

"Argentina?"

"Right. And then from there we'll fly to . . . how about Spain? Neither of us made it there, and surely we will have learned Spanish after all that time in South America."

"Yeah! And then we can go to Hungary and into Turkey and Lebanon . . ."

"And then maybe Russia?" I asked hopefully.

"That's not very close to Lebanon. I was thinking we could go through Israel and into Egypt to see the Pyramids and then Jordan to see Petra. We can do Africa and then up to India and Nepal . . ."

"And then Indonesia!"

"Indonesia's nowhere near Nepal. I was thinking more Tibet and then China and then Southeast Asia."

"And then Hawaii?"

"Uh . . . Hawaii's not actually close to anything." She paused. "You really need to look at a map."

Our original plan included some fifty countries, which was very exciting until Sara realized it would take us three years and seventy thousand dollars apiece. So we took an axe to it. Central and South America were out because they would take too long. Europe and the Middle East were out because they were too expensive, and China was out because it was too big. Hawaii, apparently, had never been *in*. Finally, we settled on southern Africa, Nepal, Tibet, India, and Southeast Asia, and allotted ourselves a year and twenty thousand dollars each.

Our parents' reactions to the idea ranged wildly. At one end of the spectrum was Sara's father, who had spent nearly two years on the road in the seventies and was elated that his daughter was following in his footsteps. However, his response was subdued by Sara's mother, who was at the opposite end of the scale. Jean was a momma hen, keen on keeping her chicks under her wing, and guarding them with wary eyes and a sharp beak. Needless to say, the idea of her daughter traveling around the world was enough to ruffle her feathers.

"*Sara!* Are you *crazy?* Do you know what's *out* there?" Jean's hands fluttered around her face. "Isn't it enough that we lent you the money to go to *Europe?* We thought you would have this traveling business out of your *system* by now! I just read this article about that place and—"

"Which place, Mom?" Sara interrupted. "I haven't even told you where we're going yet."

"I read articles about *lots* of places! Oh, I *never* expected this kind of *trouble* from *you!*"

It was painstaking convincing Jean that this was neither (a) a post-teenage crisis leading to drug experimentation and a pierced tongue nor (b) a pursuit that would result in her daughter being shipped home in a box. But eventually they reached a compromise: Sara was allowed to go as long as she didn't visit any "questionable" countries.

"What's a 'questionable' country?" I asked.

Sara shrugged. "Who knows?" She laughed and added, "Hey, I've been so good for so long. Everyone's allowed to rebel a little, right?"

I really couldn't picture Sara rebelling—the girl used *book-marks*—but I wasn't about to contradict her. Fortunately, my parents' response was far more amicable than Jean's.

"I'm *so* glad you have faith in my decision-making skills," I said with relief.

"Uh, sure. You're going to be with Sara the *entire* time, right?" said Mom. "Don't even wander off to the bathroom without her. In fact, it's probably best if you just tried not to pee altogether."

"Let her organize *everything*," added Dad. "I don't want you writing anything down. Remember when you came home from Europe and started writing your ones like sevens, and the mess that caused?"

And so it was settled. Sara planned, I daydreamed, Jean worried. Lists were made and revised. Plane tickets were purchased. Backpacks were dragged out of storage and secretly worn around the bedroom. Shopping trips were continuous as we scoured the city for everything from the most comfortable hiking boots to the most deadly mosquito repellant. The countdown of months dwindled into weeks, and then days. And then hours. And then I freaked out.

THE DAY WE were due to leave, I woke up with what felt less like butterflies in my stomach and more like a pack of snarling weasels. For the first time, the magnitude of what we were about to do hit me with full force. Was I a fucking *idiot*? Here I was—the twenty-three-year-old waitress who *still lived with her parents*—about to go run amok through the great unknown without adult supervision. What made me think I was *capable* of this? Thinking about it now, I wasn't capable of very much. I couldn't graduate from university. I couldn't parallel park. Just last week, I'd nearly burned the house down while scrambling eggs. Jean was right—we were going to die. Well, I was going to die. Sara could run faster than me, so she might live. Whose stupid idea was this, anyway?

I was so rattled that I accidentally ate breakfast twice and forgot to shave one leg. I alternated between hot flashes and cold sweats, and compulsively unpacked and repacked my backpack six times just to make sure I had everything.

"Shit, I forgot my toothbrush!" I cried, frantically flinging socks and underpants over my shoulder as I dug out my toiletries bag.

"You have your toothbrush," said Mom. "Look, you've crossed it off your list."

"Just because I crossed it off the list doesn't mean it's in here!"

"I saw you put in it there. Remember? You ran into the bathroom to grab it when I was on the toilet because you couldn't wait two freaking minutes . . ."

"Oh, you don't know what you saw!" I snapped. "See? It's not even . . . oh, wait. Here it is." I took a deep breath. "Sorry. I'm just a little nervous."

"I know you are, dear."

"Crap, did I remember aspirin? I know I've checked it off but . . ."

She kissed the top of my head. "I'm going to go make you some tea."

When we met up at the airport, I saw that Sara wasn't doing much better than I was. Her anxiety, evident from her trembling lip, was surpassed only by Jean's—who looked as though she was on the verge of throwing a temper tantrum. We made small talk over airport food that nobody wanted, laughed at jokes that weren't funny, and tried to keep each other calm.

Then, it was time. Dad told me to have fun; Mom reminded me to listen to Sara; Sara's dad told her he was proud of her gumption; her mom said there was still time to change our minds, surely the cost of the flight was no great loss compared to a lesson learned, and we could all go home and laugh about this in the morning. Or something like that. With a round of tearful hugs and one last forlorn wave across airport security, we were finally On Our Own.

As we rounded the corner toward the departures lounge, Sara and I burst into nervous giggles.

"That was intense," she said.

"No kidding."

"How do you feel?"

I thought about it. "I've been going bananas all day, but now . . . strangely enough, I feel okay."

"Me too. I think we can do this."

"I fucking hope so."

- 1 -
How to Not Get Eaten by Lions
(and Other Africa Survival Tips)

FEBRUARY: SOUTH AFRICA, NAMIBIA,
BOTSWANA, ZIMBABWE

One of the Barbies: *Sooooo, the lion's, like, the boy and the tiger's the girl, yah?*

W E ARRIVED IN Cape Town exhausted and stinking—
which, I'd soon discover, would become a prevalent
theme over the next ten months. Bleary-eyed, we claimed
our backpacks and hailed a cab. As we whizzed down the empty
highway beneath the copper glow of the streetlamps, I thought
back to a comment a mutual friend had made when we told her
we were beginning our adventure in South Africa.

"Oh yeah, Cape Town—my cousin went there on her honey-
moon. They got stabbed."

"But that was in the middle of the night and they were in a
dark alley, right?" prompted Sara.

"Nah, they were on Table Mountain and it was like two in the
afternoon." She paused. "It was just a flesh wound, though. They
were fine after surgery."

Jet lag riddled our brains and for the first few days we felt like
zombies who'd spent too much time on the spinning teacups. But
even our lurching and disoriented state couldn't eclipse the beauty
of Cape Town. We had departed Toronto on the last day of January
amid snow mounds that were once Nissans and temperatures that
plunged to bone-rattling frigidity. But in the southern hemisphere
the sun was glorious, sparkling off the waves and turning our
bikini-clad bodies vermillion as we scrambled for shade.

You flew 13,000 km to go to the beach? wrote Dad in an email.
Florida would've been cheaper, you know.

You should be proud, we're playing it safe, I replied. *As I'm
sure Jean would be eager to tell you, South Africa's got edge.
It's not exactly the place for two unassuming twenty-three-
year-old girls to be gallivanting around like Carmen Sandiego.
Which is why we have decided to gently ease ourselves into this*

adventure-travel thing. After all, this trip is about becoming self-sufficient, answerable adults capable of holding our own anywhere in the world—not doing crazy stuff just for the hell of it.

Dad answered, *Well, Daughter, I am impressed. Here I was thinking you two had just run away to get your kicks. Sara must be a good influence. It's only been four days and yet it sounds like you're maturing already.*

"I take it you didn't tell him we're going cage diving with great white sharks, then?" Sara asked as she read over my shoulder.

"I was thinking of saving that for my next email."

Located an hour and a half from Cape Town is Gansbaai, a world-renowned hot spot for great whites. It was here that any soul with the fortitude to stare danger in the gnashing teeth (and with at least two hundred dollars on their credit card) could climb into a cage and float next to the most iconic, fearsome, and blood-lusting predators of the sea. I *had* to do it. Just think of the Facebook status!

"Are you sure about this?" asked Sara as I dragged her to the registration office and threw a wad of money at the front desk. "Haven't you seen *Jaws*?"

"I've seen *Jurassic Park* too, and that hasn't stopped me from going into the forest."

"Well, obviously, but that's because—oh, never mind." She shook her head. "All I'm saying is that we're going to have a lot of opportunities to do fringe stuff. We don't have to risk our lives *every* chance we get."

"Now what kind of an attitude is that?" I dropped the unread waiver I'd been about to sign and whirled around to face her. "I thought this trip was about pushing our limits. Facing our fears. Triumphing over that which others pale at. But if you're going to pussy out over the first wee bit of danger . . . well, maybe we should just go to a *museum* instead."

"For heaven's sakes—give me that!" She snatched up the waiver and scrawled her name at the bottom. "My mother is going to kill me."

"As long as it's your mother and not the sharks—oh my god, I'm *so kidding!*"

The next day we were up at five AM, crusty eyed and jittery bellied. After being driven to Gansbaai and given a safety briefing, we were led aboard the boat. It was small, with a capacity of about twenty passengers, and it bounced wildly on the rolling waves. The cage was attached to the side—six feet long, three feet wide, and tall enough that we could float vertically inside. The bars connected to form yawning ten-inch squares and were made from the most indestructible, unyielding, apocalypse-proof metal in the world. Or so they told us. The idea was for us to climb into the cage wearing masks and snorkels and hang on to the bars to keep our heads above water. Once a shark was spotted, someone on the boat would holler the cue and we'd plunge underwater in order to go snout to snout with what was surely nature's Aston Martin of predators.

As fortune would have it, Sara and I were selected to go first. But as we wiggled into our wetsuits and clambered into the cage, my confidence began to wane. The water was breathtakingly cold and murky with recent plankton blooms. We seesawed in the massive swell and struggled to keep our flippered feet inside the cage as the waves clanged discordantly against the boat. My mask began to fog over and everything took on a surreal, wraithlike appearance. And it was while we were bobbing there like vulnerable corks on the sea of time that the reality of the situation finally sank in.

I was in the middle of the ocean. Surrounded by great white sharks. Separated from a gruesome fate by a couple of flimsy rods spaced *way too fucking far apart!*

Well, that was it then. I was going to die.

My heart thrashed so wildly in my chest I thought it was going to launch itself out of my body and back onto the boat. This was like some sort of idiotic game of chicken in which you see how near you can get your hand to a flame—except instead of just singeing a fingernail, you risk your arm being wrenched from its socket and devoured before your eyes as you bleed out and drown. If we died today, our mangled corpses would be a small victory for Darwinism.

"Sara," I battled to retain my composure. "I . . . uh . . . I'm going to sit this one out."

"Excuse me?" she muffled through her snorkel.

"I've just realized how incredibly stupid we are. I think we should climb out, dry off, wait for *Shark Week* on Discovery Channel, and never speak of this again."

"You're not funny."

"I'm not trying to be. Maybe you don't fully grasp the situation—there are *sharks swimming all around us* right now. In fact, the people on the boat are *actively beckoning them forth*. We have to *get out of here!*" I paused. "What would your mother say?"

"Oh you did *not* just—"

"*Shaaaaaark!*" somebody yelled. "Quick! Go under!"

Sara plunged her face into the water, and without thinking, I did the same. At first, all I could see was the greenish ether of the ocean. But then, I caught a glimpse of a gray flank, a white belly, a fin, a snout, a black eye—*a shark!* Just three feet from us! And then, like a mirage, it vanished.

Seconds later, we popped up whooping.

"Holy shit!" I yelled. "Did you see that? Did you freaking *see that?*"

"Heck yeah I did!" Sara exclaimed. "A great white—"

"*Shaaaaaark!*"

Between the limited visibility in the water and the confines of the diving mask, watching the great whites underwater was a warped experience. They appeared in glimmers, filling our vision with slivers of body parts—theirs, fortunately, not ours—and then disappearing from view in an undeterminable direction. This was nothing like standing back and gazing into an aquarium. It was flashes of action embedded against marine nothingness, forcing us to piece together the image of the thunderous fish too large to be captured in one glance.

By the time we hauled ourselves back on deck, we were practically delirious. Exhilaration like champagne bubbles fizzed and popped in our brains. We collapsed in a heap, panting and babbling as the boat continued to pitch.

"At first you couldn't see anything because the visibility was so poor—"

"And then it was just this gray—"

"—coolest thing *ever*!"

"Wait, look! You can see them from here!"

As it turned out, the view from the boat was much better than that from the water. Now we could tell that the sharks were well over fifteen feet long. Sara and I watched in awe as they breached the water, their razor teeth ripping like chainsaws into the floating entrails that had been tossed overboard. We grinned at each other again.

After a moment, though, Sara's smile began to fade. "Is it just me or is this boat really rocky?" she asked. I noticed her lips had blanched.

"Tell me about it. I feel like a T-shirt in the spin cycle. Just tumbling round and round and—"

As if on cue, a woman pushed past us and flung herself at the railing, puking violently into the churning sea. It was then that I realized we were surrounded by wet-suited individuals hurling chunks over the side of the boat. My stomach, which had finally unwound itself, now began to flutter dishearteningly.

"Uh-oh," I said. "Did you bring any motion sickness tablets with you? Sara? Sara!"

But she was too busy chumming the water with her own revisited breakfast to reply.

AFTER MUCH DELIBERATION, we had decided to explore Africa as part of a tour. Our reasoning was that Africa was (a) big and (b) scary, and while it would earn us crazy backpacker points to venture forth as two skinny white chicks going stag, there was a fair chance we'd end up raped and murdered. And not necessarily in that order.

That said, we were determined not to go on any sort of Contiki-style "vacation." To hell with plush hotels, gourmet meals, and chicks with wheelie suitcases that traveled on Daddy's credit card. Just because we wanted an organized tour didn't mean we couldn't get our hands dirty. And so we picked an Africa-based company that led rugged camping trips into remote corners of the continent. We would be sleeping in tents, barbecuing dinner, and running through the bush after all sorts of large, harrowing creatures that wanted to eat our faces. In short, we would be *real* backpackers. The tour would begin in Cape Town and weave through Namibia, Botswana, and Zimbabwe before ending in Johannesburg twenty-four days later.

Before we left home, we extended an invitation to anybody who wanted to join us for a leg of our trip. Kendra, Sara's roommate from university, jumped at the chance. She arrived in Cape Town shortly after we did and just in time for the meet-and-greet on the night before the tour began.

"What do you think the others will be like?" Sara asked as we walked toward the restaurant.

"I bet they'll be mostly French or German guys in their late twenties," I predicted. "Intelligent yet adventurous, with really expensive cameras. And at least three of them will be super hot."

Kendra laughed. "You wish. I think there's going to be a couple of aging UCLA prof types who know the names of every plant species and what happens if you smoke them."

"Nah, you're both way off," said Sara. "Watch: Japanese tourists with compasses, safari hats, and ten thousand moist towelettes."

"I hope you're wrong," said Kendra. "Although after twenty-four days in the wilderness, we'll probably be aching for moist towelettes."

Laughing, we entered the restaurant. And then dropped our jaws accordingly.

Twelve barely legal blond girls in stiletto heels and cocktail dresses chatted in a language that sounded like English spoken backward. They circled like Playboy buzzards around what I presumed to be our guide, a burly guy in his late twenties sporting a ginormous grin. One of them tried to catch his eye while nibbling seductively on a maraschino cherry. Three others appeared to be drunk even though we hadn't ordered dinner yet. When we walked in, nobody looked up.

"Wha . . . I . . ." stammered Kendra. "That is *not* proper jungle attire!"

Indeed it was not. I eyed the Barbie safari with contempt. Where were the three hot French and/or German guys? Where was the hippie-scientist to smoke us on some desert green? How on earth were these bimbos going to survive in the bush? Did Gucci even make galoshes? More importantly, would they sneer at my waist-length dreadlocks and ratty blue jeans? We sat down and smiled politely as the obligatory round of introductions was made.

"So, do you all know one another or something?" Sara asked.

"No, but like, oh my *god*, we're *all* from Norway and we *all* just graduated from high school! What a chance, *yah*!" exclaimed one of the girls in an accent that bounced as if she was riding on a horse. Her breasts jiggled in a similar manner. She then said something in Norwegian, and everybody laughed—except for us and the guide.

What was that about no chicks with wheelie suitcases that traveled on Daddy's credit card?

"Drinks?" the waitress appeared at my shoulder.

"Oh, I'm just going to have a wa—"

"Vodka/soda," interrupted Kendra.

Sara and I exchanged glances. "Actually, make that three." Turning to our guide, I said, "I'm sorry, I didn't catch your name."

"Charrrrrlie," he boomed, his Afrikaans "R" rolling like a marble on a roulette table. He was tall and broad-shouldered, with hands the size of frying pans and a face ruddy from too much sunshine. "Miss!" he called to the waitress. "Another double gin and tonic for me, *dankie*!"

"That's his third so far," whispered one of the Barbies.

When the waitress returned with our drinks, Charlie lifted his high in the air and proposed a toast.

"To the jungle!" said Kendra, raising her glass.

"To the party!" cried another one of the Barbies.

"To the good time!" thundered Charlie, grinning even wider.

"Uh . . . cheers?" Sara and I knocked our glasses together, exchanged another worried glance, and slammed back our drinks.

THERE'S NOTHING LIKE starting an African safari with a hangover. It was gray and drizzling and miserable outside—weather that felt as poorly as we did. Dressed in jogging shorts and hoodies, Sara, Kendra, and I sat on the curb and waited for the bus to pick us up.

"Ugh, I hope we don't see any zebras today," groaned Kendra.

"Why not?" I asked.

"I don't think I can handle all those black and white stripes running around. I'm nauseous enough as it is." She popped a couple of chewable stomach tablets into her mouth and her teeth turned bright pink.

"Team Canada, is the bus here yet?"

The Barbies arrived, looking as primped and plastic as ever. They wore lacy sundresses and enough makeup that a mosquito landing on their cheek would sink into the goo and fossilize. The Cover Girl tar pits, indeed.

"You've *got* to be kidding me," muttered Kendra. "Is that one in heels?"

As I self-consciously reapplied my ChapStick, a vehicle that could only be described as the choice camper van for the apocalypse rumbled toward us. It was army green and mean looking, with tires that came up to my chest. There were large windows on top and metallic drawers underneath big enough to hold food, camping supplies, and Connecticut.

Sara whistled. "That is some bus."

The door swung open and a small ladder clanged to the ground. Sitting at the wheel with a wide-brimmed hat on his head and a cigarette dangling from his sun-blistered lips was Charlie. "It's not a bus," he corrected her as we scrambled aboard. "It's a truck."

The rain eased up but the mist hung heavy as the truck lumbered down the city streets. I popped two aspirins and one of Kendra's stomach tablets, and sank down low in my seat. Three days of shark lag and jet diving were finally catching up with me. Despite not wanting to miss anything (even if it was just suburbia), I allowed my eyelids to droop as my seat gently lolled with the curves of the road.

When I woke up, the clouds had vanished and the arm I'd rested on the window ledge was sizzling in the sun. I yawned and peered outside. The suburbs had given way to rocky desert strewn with dusty, low-lying brush. It stretched out in all directions until the horizon was no more than a brownish-blue smudge. The sky was deep cobalt and looked higher and more important than the sky back home. Distant hills were dotted with fairy circles—a yet-to-be-explained phenomenon in South Africa and Namibia where perfectly round bald patches appeared in the brush. It was sort of like the African equivalent of crop circles, except here it was way too hot for anybody to get that wound up over it.

I spent the next many hours gazing out at the lonely two-lane highway. After a while, it felt like we were characters in a cheap cartoon passing by the same background over and over again. The dusty, archaic nothingness went on *forever*. And although we were only a hundred-some-odd miles away from civilization, I couldn't shake the humbling yet terrifying sensation of extreme middle-of-nowhereness—as if the desert were swallowing me up like just another grain of sand.

It was late enough in the day that the sunlight had softened from gold to rose when we finally pulled off the highway. We parked in what I would have sworn was an arbitrary field amid red boulders and scrubby bushes had it not been for the singular toilet protruding conspicuously from the ground.

"We're here!" announced Charlie.

"Could've fooled me," muttered Kendra.

We climbed out and stretched our cramped, sticky limbs. Sara set up our tent while Kendra and I pretended to do useful things with poles and zippers. Dassies, which are rodents similar to guinea pigs, scurried in the bushes nearby. Charlie found a scorpion and picked it up by the tail to show us ("Isn't that dangerous?" "For me, like a bee sting. For you . . . just don't touch it.") and then made a bonfire while we prepared dinner. As everybody ate, he regaled us with stories of growing up in rural Pretoria—childhood bush games of plucking hairs from elephant tails and seeking refuge in trees from irate rhinos—while nonchalantly downing a twelve-pack of beer.

Finally, our eyes grew weary and we succumbed to the night. It was only nine thirty, but we were exhausted. We brushed our teeth by the light of our headlamps and tried not to spit on the dassies. Then we said our goodnights and crawled into our tents.

"Has the ground always been this hard?" I asked as I tried to find a position that minimized the number of rocks digging into my soft bits.

"Is that a rhetorical question?" Kendra pulled her sleep mask over her eyes.

"I don't know what you're complaining about. I'm comfortable," said Sara. "Now please stop kicking and go to sleep." As if leading by example, she rolled over and was out cold immediately. Kendra soon followed suit. Thus I was alone to contend with the passive-aggressive rocks beneath my sleeping bag, the desert flies buzzing around my head, and the things that went bump in the night.

And bump they did go.

I had almost dozed off when a rustle in the darkness brought me back to consciousness. What was that? A scorpion? A jaguar? Whatever it was, it sounded like it was right outside the tent. Buggy of eye and tense of jaw, I held my breath to see what would happen. After a few moments of silence, I exhaled tentatively. It was probably nothing. Just a dassie blowing in the wind. Or something like that.

I rolled over and tried to relax. *Everything's fine*, I told myself. Just because we were in the middle of the desert a gazillion miles away from anything, where the only rules are that of the wild, of hunter and prey, of eat or be eaten, didn't mean we were necessarily in danger. After all, we were in a nylon tent! It would take the jaguar forever to figure out the zipper.

Suddenly, another noise rang out through the darkness—a loud screeching sound—and I sat bolt upright, whacking my head on one of the poles in the process. That was definitely *not* a dassie blowing in the wind. I stared expectantly at Sara and Kendra, waiting for them to wake up and join me in my petrified huddle. But they remained asleep, and the sound did not come again. A few minutes later, I yawned and lay back down.

This time what brought me back from the brink of dreamland was not a bump in the night but a pang in my bladder. Crap—I *knew* I shouldn't have drunk that much water! I tried to convince myself to hold it until daybreak. However, when I checked my watch, I was dismayed to discover that we'd been in bed only an hour. That meant another seven to go before dawn. After much deliberation, I decided the only thing worse than facing the desert alone would be waking up to discover that I'd turned my sleeping bag into my very own moist towelette. So I grabbed my headlamp, rolled out of my sleeping bag, and unzipped the flap—ready to take on the night.

Well, almost. I spent a solid five minutes staring into the abyss before I mustered the courage to actually leave the tent. Then I spent another two standing just outside with my feet jammed into my sandals, waiting to see if was going to be tackled and eaten by some sort of night stalker. I probably would have stood there forever if my bladder hadn't given another kick, forcing me to venture forth. I didn't even try for the toilet—after having walked what I considered to be a sanitary enough distance from the tent, I pulled down my pajamas, squatted, and watered the soil.

A low rumbling snarl nearly knocked me over.

I froze, both fight and flight instincts abandoning me as I crouched, terrified, about to die alone and bare-assed. *What the fuck was that?* After a moment, it came again, slowly and rising to a crescendo before fading away. I frantically looked about but my headlamp didn't catch any hungry eyes or carnivorous teeth.

In fact, the only thing I could see was a nearby tent that I remembered belonged to Charlie.

Charlie! He'd know what to do. If only I could make it to his tent before I was mauled and shredded to a bloody pulp . . . Gingerly, so as not to draw attention to myself, I pulled up my pajamas and inched forward, my heart hammering. But as I reached for the zipper, the rumbling snarl came again. *From inside Charlie's tent.*

This time I really did fall over—bowled backward by sheer terror and the fact that my sandals weren't on properly. The beast was inside Charlie's tent! It was probably gnawing on his flesh at that very moment! It must have somehow figured out the zipper . . . and then zipped it back shut after it had gotten in . . . and then . . .

Wait a second.

Well, that was embarrassing.

I quietly picked myself up, dusted myself off, and returned to my sleeping bag. As I stared at the nylon ceiling, I felt comforted by the notion that Charlie's bestial snores would probably keep the real animals at bay. That said, there was a part of me—a tiny, irrational part that had eaten too many Extreme Doritos as a child—that was disappointed there hadn't been any terrifying creatures skulking in the shadows. The sensation of adrenaline gurgling through my veins was kind of neat. And hey, I'd handled the sharks fairly well—certainly a lion couldn't be *that* much more challenging.

Oh well. Surely there would be other opportunities to take on the wildlife in the coming weeks. In the meantime, I desperately needed to shake my jet lag, and thus rolled over and shut my eyes.

WE AWOKE THE next morning to discover that the rising sun had transformed our little tent into a Crock-Pot, stewing us in our own juices. Sleepily, we packed up camp and were on our way. As we crossed the border into Namibia, our blacktop highway gave way to a dirt road so indiscernible from the surrounding desert I wondered if we were still actually adhering to it or if Charlie had just picked a direction and was hoping for the best.

Animals began to appear. At first it was only a smattering along the horizon that might have just been flies crawling on the windshield, but as we made our way from the infertile dust to the grassier plains, they became abundant. Ostriches pecked at the ground, fluffy and gauche like upturned feather dusters. Springbok grazed in massive herds, pronging—a bouncy, straight-legged gait that reminded me of the walk-run kids did when scolded for running in the hallways—whenever the truck rolled too close. Zebras flicked their tails and watched for lions like hundreds of skittish Foot Locker employees. Weaverbirds spun ornate nests in the trees while giraffes, gemsbok, and wildebeests reposed in the shade.

After a few nights on the hazy grasslands of Namibia, we headed to the marshier terrain of Botswana. Twiggy yellow brush sprouted into disheveled green bush and then became a living wall of palms, vines, and thorns. The bold skies and crackling heat were replaced by unfurling clouds and humidity that made us feel like we'd accidentally stepped into a mouth. If I had thought that nighttime was loud before, nothing prepared me for the orchestra of songs and screams, of caws and crashes, of buzzes, of growls, of snapping twigs and ominous rustles that echoed outside the tent. And this time, the noise wasn't just Charlie.

To our utmost surprise and delight, we arrived at a campsite that not only was more than just an arbitrary piece of ground, but also actually had a tiki bar. Sara, Kendra, and I hurriedly set up our tent and dumped our bags, then went over for drinks. After all, those desert days hadn't been easy. We were often awake before the first lavenders of dawn, and hiking in forty-degree weather was exhausting. Plus, there were tents to be pitched, meals to be prepared, and rocks to be slept on. It was awesome, of course, but it was also nice to chill out with a cocktail while listening to Afro-pop and sitting on actual chairs.

Outside, the clouds boiled over; torrents of rain poured down amid the crackle-and-boom of thunder and lightning. But under the tiki roof, the party was just getting started. There were shots, followed by more shots, followed by Kendra shimmying under a leak in the roof and me gyrating on the bar until Charlie lifted me down. We had a drink for the giraffes, and a drink for the ostriches, and another drink for the giraffes because we forgot we had already done them. And by that time everybody was so obliterated we had a drink for that too.

When Sara and I finally went back to our tent (Kendra having passed out long ago across a couple of chairs), we'd lost all track of time and at least one sandal. We held hands as we stumbled down the muddy pathway with rain and branches in our eyes, eager to sleep away the spins. But when we climbed into our tent, we discovered that something had gone disastrously awry.

"Ssssara," I slurred, "Did we always have a lake in our tent, or is that a new addition?"

"Um . . ." She squinted. "No, no this definitely wasn't here before."

"I see. What is our course of action?"

"I don't know, but my clothes are wet from the walk. Let's put on our pajamas and then decide."

"Okay."

Trying not to fall into the murky jungle water—which was up to our ankles—we stripped down to our underpants and dropped our shorts and T-shirts to the floor of the tent. They were instantly submerged.

"Good," said Sara. "Now to get on some dry clothes. Where are our backpacks?"

"Underwater."

"Right. Wait a sec. What?"

We looked at each other. Suddenly, light bulbs went on above our heads (literally, as we were in fact wearing headlamps) and illuminated the obvious point that we'd drunkenly missed.

"Dammit!" Sara cried. "Dammit crap *shit*!"

"What are we going to *do*?" I wailed. "I don't *want* to sleep underwater! It's cold and I don't have a snorkel!"

We swore and hopped and yelled at the water in our best Old Testament voices in vain hopes that it would make a retreat. After we had tired ourselves out, we decided that our best bet was to go sleep in the truck. Thankfully Charlie had left it unlocked, and we managed to climb inside with a minimal number of scrapes and stubbed toes. The storm had cooled things down, however, and we were beginning to shiver in our rain-wet underwear. With my drunken buzz rapidly morphing into a hangover headache, I grabbed a sweatshirt lying on one of the seats and pulled it over my head.

"That's not yours," said Sara.

"I don't care. I'm soaked, I'm freezing, and this smells pleasantly of vanilla."

She considered my logic, then picked up a nearby sarong and wrapped it around herself. We bunked down in the seats and closed our eyes, but sleep was still elusive. The relentless rain defied all rules of decorum and continued to plague us even within the refuge of the vehicle.

"Sara?"

"Mmm?"

"Why is it raining *inside* the truck?"

"I think there's a leak. Or two. Or twelve."

"Motherfucker. What do we do?"

"I don't know, are there any more clothes?"

When Charlie found us the next morning, we were bundled up like nesting dolls in layers of backward/inside out clothing—damp, sniffling, hungover, and cranky.

"Is that my top?" one of the Barbies asked. Then she saw my expression and quickly added, "Because you can totally borrow it. Looks good on you. Accentuates your eyebrows."

Upon daylight examination, we found that Kendra's backpack had avoided the worst of the flooding and about half of Sara's stuff was salvageable. Everything in my bag, however, was drenched. My journal was runny and wrinkled, my soap had bubbled away into oblivion, and my hiking boots were cultivating some sort of primordial pond scum. The worst part was that we were about to leave so there was no time for us to string up a clothesline to dry out our stuff. And while Kendra and Sara weren't as badly off as I was, they were in no position to lend anything out, either.

"*Shit*," I muttered to no one in particular as I wrung the water out of my pants. "Now what am I going to do?"

"I was serious when I said you could borrow my top," said the Barbie whose shirt I was wearing. Her name was Astrid. "It's no big deal. I have plenty."

"And I have a pair of khakis for you," added her friend Karin. "I've only worn them once. They make my hips look big."

A third girl, Grete, chimed in, "I have an extra sundress. I mean, I know it is not your thing, *yah*, but at least it's dry."

As it turned out, the Barbie safari had brought so much clothing—"you never know when you need a waist-belt, *yah*!"—that it was nothing to them to part with a couple of articles. I couldn't believe it. One minute, I'd been soaking and miserable, and the next I was warm and dry. And perhaps a little glitzier than I'd intended to be, but I couldn't complain. Suddenly, I felt guilty about secretly harping on about their excessive wardrobes.

"Wow! Thanks!"

"It's nothing. Besides, to be honest, you needed a bit of a makeover," said Karin. I gasped and she laughed. "I'm joking! Grunge is totally making a comeback."

No wonder Barbie has so many friends—she's a pretty cool chick, I thought. Instead of saying that out loud, I looked down sheepishly. "This is seriously wicked of you guys."

Of course, there was still the issue of what to do with all of our damp clothing. If we kept it in our backpacks, it would just rot away. But that left us with only one option. And so, we proceeded to cruise down the African highway with every garment we owned—shirts, pants, bras, shorts, sarongs, towels, sleeping bags, socks, and underwear—flapping out the windows of the truck, much to the incredulous wonder of onlooking locals and wildlife.

Our primary stop in Botswana was the Okavango Delta, the swampy backwoods where the Big Five roamed. The Big Five (elephant, lion, buffalo, rhino, and leopard) were so named for being the most difficult and dangerous animals to hunt on foot. It was treacherous territory. Unlike Namibia's savannah, which was mostly home to grazers and gallopers, the delta housed all sorts of vexing creatures known for trampling, mauling, impaling, and snacking on human flesh. My mild apprehension (okay, okay, total panic attack) during that first night's pee run seemed foolish in retrospect. That had been nothing, a mere stroll in the dust. This was Africa at its most feral and fierce.

We were going to need a better truck. We abandoned our fuck-off rapture machine for its smaller, sleeker cousin—a truck-jeep hybrid that looked as though it could climb trees. It plunged through orange rivers and bounded over fallen trees with chutzpah. Eventually, we came to a tall wire fence (the official entrance into the Okavango) where we picked up our guides—tough-looking men who had grown up in traditional villages on the delta's edge.

"What's the fence for?" asked Sara.

"It's a Big Five fence," explained one of the guides.

I regarded it warily. It looked to me like they were trying to hold back a stampeding elephant with grandma's knitting. "Does it actually *work*?"

He shrugged. "Eh. Sometimes."

We passed through the fence and headed deep into the heart of the delta. It got darker, both from the swelling clouds and from the shadows cast by the dense canopy. As we set up camp, I felt goose bumps on the back of my neck as I couldn't help but wonder what was lurking in the bushes, watching us and licking its chops.

Our first excursion took place in the water aboard *mekoros*— small dugout canoes carved from single trees. It was two of us to a mekoro, plus a guide who stood at the back and pushed us along with a long pole, much as a Venetian gondolier does. Lilies the size of soup bowls blanketed the water, their periwinkle petals and golden centers hyper-vivid against the charcoal sky. Tall grasses housed tiny calico frogs no bigger than the tips of our fingers. Birds sang and cried from the trees as unseen insects chirped.

"Look," whispered our guide, dragging his pole to stop the mekoro and pointing toward a flat expanse of open water. "Hippopotamuses!"

About a hundred yards away, three small dark humps sat low in the water. They were almost indistinguishable from the flotsam save for their comically little ears, which twitched to keep the flies away.

"Hippos actually kill more people every year than all of the Big Five combined," he explained. "They are very cantankerous and will charge if provoked. I have known lots of people who have been killed by hippos."

As if on cue, one of the hippos yawned to reveal a massive pink mouth with four gigantic incisors, then emitted a noise that was a cross between a snort and a bellow.

"He really does look hungry-hungry," whispered Kendra.

As we continued our journey across the marsh, the hippos watched us, their snouts lurking below the water line. I thought about what it'd be like to be killed by a hippo—ravaged by a hybrid between a giant pig and an overturned bathtub, with teeth the size of salt shakers and the temperament of a wet cat—and shuddered deliciously. Every now and again we'd spot another one, and our guides would discreetly shift our course in order to give the pachyderms a wide berth, although I silently wished we could drift just a *little* bit closer.

"What's that?" asked Sara. "I thought it was a log, but it just moved."

"Crocodile," said her guide. "Not quite as bad as the hippos. I do have friends who have lost limbs to them, though. And small children."

One of the guides said something to the others and they steered the mekoros toward the shoreline. Suddenly, there was a flurry of shrieks from above our heads. We looked up to see a group (a herd? a troop? . . . a barrel?) of large monkeys leaping excitedly among the branches, shaking the leaves at us and throwing their heads back to scream.

"Baboons," said our guide. "They're interested in us."

We stared at one another, and eventually their hollering died down. One of them even crawled down a low-hanging branch to get a better look.

"They're not afraid. They're used to humans."

"Does that mean they're tame?" asked Grete. "Like pets?"

The guide laughed. "Oh, no. Baboons are actually the most vicious ape. Their jaws are extremely powerful—second only to gorillas'. Also, they're very smart and well organized. Some people argue that they're more intelligent than chimps because they are better organized socially. But they're not as easily trained and are much more dangerous to work with."

They *did* seem intelligent. The way they interacted made me think of kids on the playground. At one point, the biggest one came quite close to us, perching on a fallen tree on the bank of the marsh. It stood up on its hind legs and struck a pose with its hip popped and its hand on its waist like an underwhelmed valley girl. Everybody in the mekoros burst out laughing.

"See?" said our guide. "He recognizes people and has done this before. He knew he'd get a reaction. We are lucky he didn't try to urinate on us."

It was bizarre to think that these primates had the high level of intelligence to recognize the same in us—as well as the subsequent potential for interaction. Certainly they weren't popping their hips for the elephants. And yet it was that anthropomorphic connection that made the idea of a baboon attack all the more terrible. That flicker of humanity suggested a little less raw instinct and a little more malicious intent.

Just then, there was a thunderous crack from the skies, and I nearly jumped out of my skin. The rains began—first as a sprinkling and then as a downpour—and I sighed to find myself yet again soaked and shivering, this time in somebody else's trousers. We made our way back to camp where Charlie had set up a tarpaulin and we huddled together to keep warm. The rain drowned out the sounds of the forest as we sat around playing a sixteen-person game of Crazy Eights, trying to keep our minds off the damp.

"Eight of clubs, change it to diamonds," said Astrid.

"I got nothing." Kendra picked up a card from the deck.

"Straight flush! I win!" exclaimed Grete as she laid down her hand, and the rest of us giggled. "What? I don't win?"

"*Faen*, Grete, what game are you playing?" Karin shook her head.

For the most part, the safari was amazing, but it certainly had its challenging moments. Like that evening, for instance. I was tired and filthy, and getting sick of campfire food. And I was worried about my wet clothing. What if it didn't dry in this weather? What if it started to mold? I pictured myself returning to the truck to discover that my socks had melted into penicillin and that my pants had sprouted life and were bullying the lesser clothing. Or (more realistically) that everything stank and nobody wanted to sit next to me on the bus. To be frank, sometimes my mind was less on the wonders of nature and more on the wonders of a bubble bath. And fluffy towels that smelled like fabric softener.

"And a king-sized bed with pillows and a duvet. Two duvets!" said Kendra when I voiced my thoughts to her.

"And an extra-large pizza."

"And waffles!"

"And a cup of tea."

"I'd *murder* for tea."

"What are you talking about?" asked Sara.

"Food, bed," I said. "How much we miss tea."

She rolled her eyes. "You *guys*! In case you haven't noticed, we're in the middle of the *Okavango Delta*. This is one of the most unique natural habitats on earth, and you're crying over *tea*?" She shook her head in disbelief.

"Aren't you cold? And wet?" I asked, embittered by her unrelenting perkiness.

"A little. But I guess these things don't bug me as much as they do you. Harden up, princess!" She gave me a good-natured poke in the ribs. I shot her a proper screw face.

The rain ceased around nightfall. Occasional drips still fell from the leaves, echoing through the forest like the syncopated footsteps of a prowling animal. The moon peered out from behind the clouds, and the droplets glistened like thousands of eyes.

"Remember," said Charlie. "This is the delta. If anybody has to take a piss, use the buddy system. Nobody goes anywhere alone in the dark."

"Great," muttered Kendra. "So now two of us will get killed instead of just one."

"Misery loves company," I said.

"Maybe if you guys didn't spend so much time thinking about tea, you wouldn't have to pee so often," suggested Sara.

We crawled into our tents and turned off our headlamps. I pulled my sleeping bag—which had fared miraculously well after a day of being whizzed down the highway—tightly around myself to protect my ears against the buzzing mosquitoes. As I slipped into a damp, troubled sleep, my mind flitted between thoughts of baths and baboons, of sipping cups and snapping crocs, of creature comforts and creatures not so comfortable. *Good night, sleep tight, don't let the bed bugs bite . . . ow, stupid bed bugs . . .*

Wait, *what?*

I sat up quickly. "Psst! Sara! Sara?"

"What?" the blanketed bundle was displeased.

"Something's biting me!"

"No it's not."

"Yes it is! I can feel it." I paused. "Multiple somethings."

"It's in your head."

"No, it's in my sleeping bag!"

"Stop whining and toughen up. And go to sleep." She rolled over and put in her earplugs.

The next morning, I woke up covered in red bites that itched so fiercely they deprived me of any pleasure I may have taken in being right.

"Sand fleas," said Charlie. "They'll live in your sleeping bag forever if you don't get rid of them."

"How do I get rid of them?" I asked, scratching frantically until Kendra swatted at my hand.

"Washing machine."

Of course. Not only were all my clothes rank but my bedding was infested with bloodsuckers too. Perfect.

"Funny, I didn't get bitten at all," said Sara brightly. "Guess I got lucky!"

I glowered.

THE VAST MAJORITY of our time in Africa was spent staring out the window of the truck. There were hikes, of course, and game drives. But we spent most days driving, our bare feet pressed up against the back of the seat in front of us and our hair frolicking as the highway air rushed in. It was too hot to talk and all of the iPods had long since run out of juice. Some of the girls read magazines while others slept, and since I wasn't very good at either on buses I just watched the world go by. It made for an interesting perspective. South Africa I now defined by the open road and nowhere and dust; Namibia was springbok; Botswana was marshy overgrowth and sheet lightning and misty patches of faraway rain; Zimbabwe was elephants and waterfalls.

The first elephant we saw was right by the road—thirteen feet tall with a broken tusk and ears that flapped like flags. It was using its trunk to strip the leaves from the trees and stuff them into its mouth. When it saw us slowing down with our cameras flashing, it turned around and gave us an eyeful of elebutt.

"The African salute," explained Charlie.

No matter—we were still ecstatic. An elephant! An actual *elephant*! Just grazing at the side of the road like a common cow. We were still squealing in at least two languages when suddenly another elephant stepped out onto the highway and Charlie had to slam on the brakes. We received our second African salute as the animal wandered down the blacktop with no concern for traffic.

"Jesus—he's all over the road!" Charlie returned the elephant's salute with one of the New York variety.

After that, it was elephant mayhem. Okay, maybe not *mayhem*, but there certainly were a lot of them. A mother and baby that retreated into the forest when they saw us approaching, an old bull with spots of pink pigmentation on the top of his head, juveniles who weren't quite tall enough to reach the leaves on the bigger trees. I couldn't believe how many there were—and we weren't even in a national park.

"Can we stop and get out?" I asked Charlie, leaning forward. "Like, next to one?"

His laugh echoed as though from below an enormous church bell. "Only if you want to end up flat like a *pannekoek*," he said, and I collapsed back in my seat with frustration.

Our last major destination in Africa was Victoria Falls. Having grown up less than two hours from Niagara Falls, Ontario, I envisioned Vic Falls to be a bustling epicenter. Which was why, upon arrival, I was somewhat surprised to learn that the last official census had listed the population as around thirty-three thousand. Our hostel was a squat stucco building behind a twelve-foot gate topped with spikes. On the other side of the dirt road was thick jungle.

Wait, what was that? Did I say *hostel*?

There was a near riot as we each scrambled to be the first off the truck and into the shower. Hair was pulled, eyes were poked, underwear was wedgied without mercy. To be honest, I was almost more stoked about the prospect of a bug-free bed than I'd been about the elephants. The sand fleas in my sleeping bag had reduced in numbers since the delta, but I was still waking up every morning with a couple of fresh bites—itchy reminders of how I was slowly being consumed in my sleep. I nearly cried with joy when I learned that, after dinner, tea would be served.

"Welcome," said the hostel manager as she dropped the room keys—like Halloween candy—into our eager hands. "We hope you enjoy your stay. We only have one rule here: *never ever* leave the compound. You see that giant gate? That will be closed, and *under no circumstances* are you to open it and venture outside."

"Because of muggers?" asked Sara.

"Well, yes, them. And also buffalo and jaguars and other wild animals."

She didn't have to tell me twice. Forget leaving the compound— I wasn't planning on leaving my bed.

Dinner was fantastic. I have no idea what it was, but it hadn't been prepared over a campfire and that was good enough for me. Afterward, there was even entertainment in the form of a traditional dance with wild gyrations and palpitating drumbeats next to a sparking fire. It was great; everything was great. I didn't even care that I was on my last set of borrowed clothes and would have to begin flipping the few pairs of underwear I'd salvaged inside out tomorrow. This was exactly what I needed to recharge. I couldn't wait to collapse into those fresh sheets and bliss out without fear of the creepies and the crawlies.

We stayed up late enjoying the performance and the tea. When it finally came time to crash, Sara, Kendra, and I returned to our shared room, where we stripped down to our sleeping attire and flung back the covers . . .

. . . only to discover that our beds were swarming with ants.

Hang on, let me rephrase that: *my* bed and *Kendra's* bed were swarming with ants—thrice-segmented devils running all over our clean sheets with their dirty feet. Sara's bed, of course, was ant free. There's no justice in this world.

"*Shit!*" cried Kendra, slapping at the bastard that was inching up her leg. "What are we going to *do*?"

"I don't know! We can't sleep here."

"Good luck with that, guys," said Sara as she pulled on her eye mask, turned over, and began snoring gently.

"Dammit," said Kendra. "I guess we should go tell the front desk?"

The front desk, however, was fast asleep—as was everybody else in the complex. Panicked, we went to Charlie's room and banged hysterically on the door until he opened up, wearing nothing but his underpants. His usual cigarette had been replaced with a large joint.

"Hello," he said as though two perturbed girls in their jammies appearing at his door at such an hour was perfectly unremarkable.

"There are ants in our bed!" whined Kendra.

"Lots of them!" I added.

"I see. Well, I've got two spare beds in this room, you're welcome to spend the night here until we get things sorted out tomorrow," he said. "Now, onto more pressing matters. Do either of you have a lighter?"

Grinning with relief, we stepped inside. His room wasn't as nice as ours—the box springs squeaked and the springs dug into our asses when we sat down—but it was better than sleeping on an anthill, and we thanked him graciously. He cracked a beer and passed the joint, and then transfixed us with stories of growing up in the bush as a daring rapscallion. We shuddered in delight as we pictured him scarcely escaping charging hippos and angry buffalo.

"Man, that is so *cool*," said Kendra, shaking her head. "I wish I had stories like that. I mean, don't get me wrong, this trip's been awesome, but I wish we could do something *really* wild, you know?"

Charlie's blue eyes glinted mischievously. He sucked back the last of the joint and dropped the still-burning cherry into an empty beer can. "Ladies," he said in a tone that rang of trouble in a most titillating way. "Fancy a walk?"

We opened his door and stepped quietly into the courtyard, looking around for any telltale reading lights glowing underneath doors. Everything was dark.

"Now, if anybody asks," said Charlie as he unlocked the padlock, unwrapped the chain, and pushed the gate along its tracks. "This never happened."

Kendra and I nodded, wide-eyed, and stood a little closer together. A part of me knew this was a terrible idea, and a montage flashed through my mind in which I was devoured by a score of wild beasts. What would it feel like to have my face torn off by a howling baboon, or my intestines feasted upon by a hungry jaguar, or my bones crushed under the hoof of a stampeding buffalo? On the other hand, what would it feel like to wander through the Zimbabwean jungle at night and survive, death tracking my every move but never attacking because . . . why? Because I was with a stoned lunatic who had previously flirted with danger so many times that, while he appeared to be privy to some sort of clandestine jungle knowledge, statistically speaking his odds of survival were becoming increasingly low.

I suddenly realized that Charlie and Kendra had already stepped out onto the dirt road, and I quickly scampered after them so I wouldn't get left behind.

The moon was waning, and whispery tendrils of clouds filtered its beams. While we could see one another clearly, the jungle looming before us was so black that colors blossomed before my eyes as I strained to see what harrowing fate awaited us in the darkness.

"Are you sure this is a good idea?" I whispered to Kendra.

"I never said that," she whispered back.

Charlie led the way and we followed about ten paces behind, abandoning all delusions of coolness and clutching each other's hands with white knuckles. Wondering whether it was true that animals could smell fear, I willed myself to calm the hell down. *It's okay*, I told myself. We had survived Africa thus far. And Charlie wouldn't be leading us out here if he truly thought we were in danger, right? After all, deep down, he was a sensible, responsible guy. *Right?*

"What's that?" asked Kendra in a low, panicked voice. She stopped. I stopped. Charlie stopped.

"What's what?"

"Those eyes . . . look! Yellow ones. Waist high. Do you see them?"

I squinted into the darkness. Was there something there? Or were her nerves just playing tricks on her?

"There's another pair! And a third! Sue, *right there!*"

Sure enough, I saw what she was looking at. There were indeed eyes glimmering in the darkness, and while we stood in the open road watching them, they were undoubtedly watching us. My knees began to tremble and my body flushed hot with surging adrenaline. Charlie held up one hand, motioning for us to stay where we were, and took a few steps forward. There was an expectant pause in which I came closer than I ever have to actually shitting my pants.

"Go!" he shouted suddenly. "Go go *gogogo!*"

We turned and bolted back toward the hostel, our flip-flops flapping as we ran. Charlie was hot on our heels and the three of us exploded into the safety of the courtyard, hyperventilating and drenched in cold sweat. He slammed the gate and wrapped the chain, clicking the padlock tightly shut.

"What . . . the hell . . ." panted Kendra, "was that?"

Charlie paused for a moment with his back to us, then turned around and forced a toothy grin. "Nothing!" he chirped, far cheerier than the moment called for. "Absolutely nothing at all. Right. Now let's go to bed and never speak of this again."

"But—"

"Do you want to go sleep with the ants?"

We fell silent.

"That's what I thought. Now, off to bed, ladies. Big day tomorrow and whatnot!"

That night, I fell asleep with visions of bloody claws dancing beneath my eyelids. When I woke up the next morning, I noticed a couple of the girls milling about on the road around where we had ventured last night.

"What are you guys looking at?" I asked.

"Lion tracks," said Karin. "You see? Paw prints in the sand."

I nearly choked on my own tongue. *Lion tracks!* I looked closer. Sure enough, there was a paw print—a *gigantic* paw print—in the fine dirt by the edge of the road. I couldn't believe it. Those eyes . . . we'd very nearly . . .

"You guys are idiots!" exclaimed Sara when we confessed to our nocturnal adventure. "Seriously. What the hell were you thinking? And Sue, don't give me this whole pushing our limits/facing our fears crap. There's a difference between pussying out and not wanting to die. You could have gotten yourself *killed*."

"Imagine the Facebook status?" was all I could think of to say.

We flew out of Johannesburg a couple of days later, exchanging contact information with Astrid, Grete, and Karin at the airport. As the sunset gleamed off of the plane's wing, Sara scarfed down her hermetically sealed spaghetti and immediately fell asleep—but I remained awake for hours catching up in my journal (which ended up being crinkled yet salvageable). It felt like I'd done more in the last thirty days than I had in the previous two decades . . . and we still had eleven months to go! Admittedly, I was no closer to deciding what to do with myself once the year was up, but there was still plenty of time for that. Instead, I had learned a very valuable lesson: facing your fears is a good idea only if those fears don't end up eating you.

- 2 -

Life is an Uphill Battle

or

Getting High With Dad

MARCH–APRIL: NEPAL

My father: *Do you think the guys from Kathmandu are called Kathmandudes?*
Sara's father: *No.*

S ARA SAT ON her bed one year prior to our departure, surrounded by a small forest of papers tattooed with underlines, circles, and margin scrawls. A stack of travel magazines marked by sticky notes in a color-coded pattern that was both systematically functional and visually pleasing had spilled onto the floor. She peered intently at her laptop screen, then sat back and clapped.

"So we've got plenty of African safari options to look at, and I've also emailed a couple of ashrams in India," she said. "As for Nepal, I talked to this guy at work and he recommended this awesome company. They're really small and basic, but he said they took care of everything—"

"Wait," I interjected. "He recommended this awesome company for what?"

"Trekking. You can't really do it by yourself. I mean, you *could*, but it's much better with porters and a guide since it's so easy to become disorientated. And we all know that if I turned you around three times in the kitchen you'd get lost."

Point taken. I stopped spinning in her desk chair. "What's trekking?"

"It's what people *go* to Nepal to *do*. There are two major routes: Everest Base Camp, which is what my dad did in the seventies, and Annapurna Base Camp. Many people do Everest just for the name, but Annapurna's been rated the best trek in the world." She gestured to her laptop. "It says here that the EBC starting point is already above the tree line, whereas ABC starts lower and travels up through lots of different ecosystems."

"Ooh, let's do that one!" I said. "But what *is* trekking, exactly?"

Sara hesitated, and it was that moment—that casual tableau of two friends in a bedroom on a cozy December afternoon—that I would look back on in a year and rue with a fervor that burned like a thousand suns. I have since learned that Sara, being the sincere person that she is, tells lies only under dire circumstances. And given the crucial nature of said lies, they tended to be *whoppers*. But at the time, I took Sara's honesty for granted. Which is why I didn't give any thought to the stumbling of her speech, or the way her eyes darted away from mine.

"A trek is like a hike," she said finally. "In fact . . . it's like a walk."

"Oh, okay. So it's not that hard then? You *know* how I feel about exercise."

"Uh . . . I'm sure it won't be too bad."

"Good." I felt reassured knowing that my long-standing conviction against strenuous activity wouldn't be compromised. "But aren't the Himalayas supposed to be, like, freezing? Because I'm not about to fly thousands of miles away just to tromp about on a snow fort when I do that here for half of the year anyway. You *know* how I feel about cold."

Sara hesitated again. "Um . . . you'll be all right, I think. Because Nepal is next to India . . . and everybody knows how hot India is . . . right?"

I nodded and resumed chair twirling. "I'm so glad you know all this. I'd be screwed without you."

She flashed me an innocent smile. "Hey, what are friends for?"

What a diabolical bitch.

SARA SAT ON her bed six months prior to our departure, the forest of papers having been clear-cut and replaced by enough medical supplies to support a small clinic in rural Mexico. She had gauze, bandages, and surgical gloves—which I found a bit ominous. She had pills for aches, colds, and a variety of bowel maladies. She had creams for any ailment that could possibly befall us: antibacterial cream, anti-inflammatory cream, rash cream, burn cream, sunburn cream, topical cream, tropical cream, ice cream, and Eric Clapton of Cream. For months she'd been stockpiling supplies, her Girl Scout self and her nurse self both working in overdrive to ensure that we had the ultimate medical kit for our trip.

"Wow, you've got enough over-the-counters there to start your own meth lab," I observed. "There's no chance of your backpack accidentally blowing up, is there?"

"It's important to be prepared—you never know what's going to happen when you're on the road. When my dad was in Nepal, his bus crashed into the side of a mountain and one guy lost an arm!"

"Let me guess: you've got a cream for that."

She sighed whimsically. "You know, that's probably the part I'm looking forward to the most."

"Losing your arm in a bus crash?"

"No, Nepal! It was my dad's favorite place. He talks about it all the time. He's so envious that I'm going. He said he would love to see the way the country's changed since he was there forty years ago."

There was an enigmatic note in her voice. But I was nauseous from spinning around in her desk chair and therefore not in the mood for a guessing game. "Say it."

"Can my dad come to Nepal with us?"

Whatever I had been expecting her to say, it wasn't that.

She mistook my silence for disdain. "Look, he doesn't have to," she said quickly. "I haven't asked him yet—obviously I was going to check with you first. I just thought that . . . never mind, it's a silly idea. Forget I said anything."

I shook my head. "No, it's not that, I was just surprised. Of course your dad can come."

"Really?" Her eyes lit up.

"Sure. It'll only be for a few weeks, and I know how much it'd mean to both of you." I laughed as she clapped gleefully. "My dad is going to be so jealous."

"Well, hang on. If my father's coming, why don't you bring yours?"

"My father? In Nepal?" While Dad had done his fair share of hippie hitchhiking in his day, he wasn't exactly a globetrotter. I wasn't even sure if he could find Nepal on a map.

"Can *you* find Nepal on a map?" Sara asked pointedly.

Crap, was that out loud?

"I guess I could bring him," I said. "He keeps saying that he wishes he did a trip like this when he was young. It's true that the most exotic place he's ever been is Scotland, but it's never too late to start, right?"

The more we talked about it, the more it sounded like a good idea. It would give us a chance to bond with them in a whole new way—by literally climbing mountains together.

"Let's do it," I said at last.

"Cool! This is going to make them *so* happy." She paused. "It's going to be a challenge for them, given their age and their health. But I'm sure they'll do fine. Besides, how hard could it be?"

And I thought the surgical gloves were ominous.

GOING FROM THE jungles of Zimbabwe to the streets of Kathmandu was like doing a line of cocaine and then getting hit in the face with a frying pan.

Narrow brick buildings leaned against one another at odd angles, held up by the collective will of the city populous. Telephone wires like tangled cat's cradles hung off poles in sparking clumps. Snaking alleyways buzzed with scrambler motorcycles, bicycle rickshaws, *tuk-tuks* (taxi vehicles that are sort of like golf carts), small cars, the occasional bovine, and cart vendors selling everything from lychees to T-shirts. Buddhist and Hindu statues peeked out from nooks and crevices adorned with marigold heads and red ash. Smudge-faced children pranced in doorways while merchants shouted, "Come look my shop!"

All this was set to a discordant symphony of horns, bells, and whistles. Nepali traffic rules dictate that the conscientious driver beeps every minute or so to alert others that he is making a turn, backing up, driving straight, or even (no lie) sitting parked. Brownouts, which plunge entire chunks of the city into darkness for six hours at a time, are the only quasi-relief from the chaos. Even those don't actually make anything less frenzied—it just means you can't see what's running you over.

For Sara, Albert (her father), Dad, and me, it was almost too much. The stench of garbage combined with the perfume of incense confused our nostrils. Dust and car exhaust stuck to our sweaty skin, streaking our faces brown. Eventually, after I had to be saved twice from the perils of oncoming traffic and once from a toxic plunge into the open sewer, we decided it was probably best to go get dinner.

We wandered into a bustling restaurant and after studying the menu—which made a valiant if not entirely successful attempt at English—we ordered a round of *momos* (vegetable dumplings) and Nepali chai. The black tea had been boiled in equal parts water and buffalo milk, then seasoned with cardamom, cinnamon, cloves, and ginger. Little did I know it would become my linchpin over the next few weeks to de-jangle myself when things got totally fucking—

But I digress.

"Here we are," said Dad as he wiped his dripping moustache. "Team Average Joe takes on the most notorious mountain range in the world."

It was an accurate description. Sara was naturally athletic and thus the most prepared of the group; I, on the other hand, had the same muscular faculty as a cheese string. Our fathers were both in their sixties. Albert was tall and lanky, soft-spoken with a British accent, and had a chronic lung condition that caused him to dissolve into terrible hacking fits. He didn't quite come off as the intrepid explorer he had been when backpacking was still in its pioneering stages. My dad was twenty pounds overweight with a cul-de-sac hairline and a compensational beard that kind of made him look like his head was on upside down. His idea of travel involved a Volkswagen bus, a map of the North American West Coast, and Pink Floyd's discography. Nepal was way out of his realm of experience.

But that didn't stop him from jumping into the experience headfirst. After dinner, he not only discovered the art of haggling, he turned it into a sport—arguing over a few rupees not because he was cheap but because of the theatrics of it (and he always allowed the shopkeepers to overcharge him anyway).

"Three hundred rupees," said the merchant when we tried to buy postcards.

"Three hundred!" cried Dad in mock horror. "I'll give you fifty."

"Two-fifty."

"Fifty or I'm going next door—and I'll pay that guy three hundred!"

The merchant blinked, unsure of how to handle this antilogic. "Uh . . . two hundred?"

Dad grabbed the merchant's hand and pumped it up and down. "You got a deal!" he grinned.

The next day, we went to find our trekking company. I expected something similar to the outfit we'd traveled with in Africa, but this business turned out to be located entirely within a small room of a house. We walked in to find a couple of worn chairs, a desk piled high with shuffled papers, and a middle-aged man with leathery skin and a massive smile.

"You must be the Coles and the Bedfords!" he said, shaking everyone's hand. "My name is Tulsi. It's great to finally meet you." After a round of introductions, we sat down to confirm the details.

"So, have you been training for this trek?" asked Tulsi.

"I've been walking around the parking lot at work for half an hour during lunchtime," said Dad proudly.

Was it my imagination, or did Tulsi's smile waver ever so slightly? "Oh . . . okay," he said. "You have all the equipment, though. Hiking poles, CamelBak water packs, quick-dry insulated layers?"

"We've brought some hats and mittens," said Albert.

"I have jeans," I added.

Tulsi laughed. "No matter," he said. "All that expensive North Face gear—it's a Westerner thing. My boys do it in flip-flops. Which reminds me." He yelled something in Nepalese, and three men appeared in the doorway.

"This is your guide, Bishwa." One of the men stepped forward.

"So, you're going to be the one to get us up that mountain, eh?" said Dad. "Tell me, is there a Tim Hortons at the top?"

Bishwa nodded, though it was obvious he didn't understand.

"He doesn't speak much English," explained Tulsi. "The other two—your porters—don't speak any at all."

The other two were our *porters*? I stared at them incredulously. They matched Sara and me in height and couldn't have weighed more than one hundred and thirty pounds each. And they were going to drag our four fifteen-kilo backpacks all the way to base camp and back? I felt a sudden pang of guilt and wished I'd packed lighter.

"Don't worry about them," said Tulsi, reading my expression. "They grew up in those foothills. This is nothing. Just be concerned about getting yourselves to the top."

"I'm not concerned," said Dad.

Again, Tulsi's smile flickered. "Of course not," he said. "I'm sure you'll be fine. After all, it's only the Himalayas."

We didn't get the joke.

FROM KATHMANDU WE traveled to Pokhara, which was the base town for many treks. The drive included hairpin turns along a narrow, cliff-edged road while trucks painted with lotus flowers passed us on both sides. Sara, Albert, and Dad were in shining moods. Sara and her father caught up on family news while Dad pressed his face against the window of the bus and squealed like a kid at everything he saw.

"Look, Sue!" he cried, pointing at a farmer's field on a plateau. "*Cabbages!* They're growing *cabbages!*"

"We've got cabbages at home, Dad." A note of impatience crept into my voice. I hadn't slept well the night before—I told TAJ (Team Average Joe) that it was because of jet lag, but the truth was that our conversation with Tulsi had made me nervous. Up until now, I hadn't given much thought toward the challenge that lay ahead. But after hearing Tulsi talk of the preparations that everybody else apparently made . . . Should we have started exercising? And what was all this gear the other trekkers were bringing? We had decent hiking boots, but otherwise we'd just brought some hand-knitted scarves and cheap hoodies.

I was especially worried about our fathers. If Sara and I didn't make it to the top, it wasn't a huge loss. We had so many other things to look forward to this year that it wouldn't be insurmountably devastating. But the dads were so excited about this. Dad bragged ad nauseam about it to anyone who would listen, and Albert's introverted self was suddenly aglow with youthful exuberance. This was their last chance to explore the world as if they were still in their twenties. I was afraid that if it didn't go well, they would feel like old, useless failures.

"Hey, want some cucumber?" Dad's voice snapped me out of my thoughts. We had pulled over to let somebody off and the vendors wasted no time in bum-rushing the bus, waving fresh cucumber slices up to the windows.

"You shouldn't eat that," I said as he passed a few rupees to outstretched hands in exchange for the snack. "Look, they've sprinkled water on it to make it look more appetizing. You know the local water isn't safe for us."

"Oh, live a little," he scoffed, biting into a slice. "Mmm, delicious."

I put on my headphones and turned up my music. *Fine, get the shits*, I thought spitefully. If he wasn't going to listen, he could learn the hard way.

We arrived in Pokhara to discover it was a haven for hippies, teeming with vegetarian cafés and shops selling Buddhist-themed souvenirs. I wondered if Nepal now overshadowed Goa as the new Mecca for tattooed nomads attempting to get high—both literally and figuratively, as I discovered after turning down three offers of hash within an hour.

The next morning—The Big Day—I awoke to find that I wasn't the only one with dark circles under my eyes. When we met for breakfast, Dad was sluggish and wan, and spilled his chai all over the table.

"Too excited to sleep, eh?" asked Sara as she grabbed some napkins to mop up the mess.

"I wish," he replied. "Nah, I was up all night with the runs. Must've been something I ate."

"That's unfortunate," she said. "Don't worry, I've got Imodium in my medical kit."

"Thanks. You're a lifesaver."

I ate my pancakes in guilty silence.

Packed and fed, we piled into a van with Bishwa and our porters and drove two hours to Phedi, the official kick-start of the trek.

I don't know what I was expecting—something notable, perhaps with a visitor's center or at least a large sign—but it turned out to be just a parking lot that was empty save for a vendor selling pop. Beyond the gravel, the cliffs began. Colossal trees grew out of the rocks at impossible angles around a zigzagging staircase of flat stones.

The porters wasted no time in taking two backpacks each, tying them together with blue twine, and hoisting them onto their backs. They set off briskly, whistling and chatting. Tulsi hadn't been kidding—they actually *were* wearing flip-flops.

"*Jum-jum!*" Bishwa turned to us. "It mean 'we go.'"

We looked at one another and exchanged thumbs-ups. It was time to take the monumental first step of a journey that really would feel like a thousand miles.

"One small step for mankind, one giant leap for Team Average Joe," said Albert.

Sara took the lead, bounding up the stairs without breaking a sweat. I came in second at a slower but steady pace. *You can do this*, I told myself. I had climbed the CN Tower for charity once, and it was one of the tallest structures in the world. This couldn't be any worse than that, right? Albert was third. He wheezed and coughed, pausing on every turn to catch his breath. But he pressed on, his tongue poking determinedly out of the corner of his mouth.

Dad, however, was in rough shape. Three flights in and he had to sit down, his face crimson. His breathing was shallow and ragged, and he was clutching at his heart in a way that filled me with terror.

"Dad!" I flew back down the stairs. "Are you okay?"

"Fuck." It was maybe the third time in my life that I'd heard him swear. "I can't . . . I just . . . shit, I'm sorry."

"It's okay, we'll go slowly!" I tried to put my arm around him, but he shrugged it off crossly. Wondering if he was actually on the verge of a heart attack, I looked up the staircase toward Sara with pleading eyes—but she was already running back to us.

"Have some water." She skidded to a stop with her bottle in her outstretched hand. "You're probably dehydrated from the diarrhea last night."

Dad thanked her and chugged it, rivulets streaming down his beard. Meanwhile, Bishwa—who had been far up ahead—doubled back to find out what was taking us so long.

"He okay?" he asked as Dad coughed and retched.

"He's fine," said Sara. "He's just dehydrated. He needs a few minutes to catch his breath, that's all."

Bishwa looked unconvinced.

After about twenty minutes, however, Dad's condition began to improve. He had finished all of his water (and half of ours) and his skin was regaining its normal hue. More importantly, he was no longer gripping his chest as if to prevent his heart from springing out.

"Okay," he said as he stood up on shaky legs. "I'm good to go. One giant leap, take two."

We set off again, this time with Albert and Bishwa up front and Sara and I lingering closer to Dad. I thought back once more to the conversation in Tulsi's office. Hadn't Sara said that Annapurna Base Camp was one of the most renowned treks in the world? People probably trained for months—and not by sauntering around the parking lot on sunny days. I hadn't done a yoga class in forever, and Dad couldn't even tackle the basement stairs without breaking a sweat. Christ, what were we *thinking*? How could we have been so blinded by our lust for adventure that we overlooked the fact that *we could not climb a fucking mountain*? We weren't Team Average Joe. We were Team Total Idiot.

As if on cue, Dad went down a second time—collapsing onto the stairs as his knees buckled beneath him.

"I just . . . a minute . . ." he gulped.

I rushed over to him while Sara ran to see if Albert had any water to spare. Meanwhile, Bishwa pulled out a cell phone and began speaking in rapid Nepalese. "Tulsi want know, he okay?" he asked, gesturing to the phone.

"Everything's fine," said Sara as she returned with more water. "Tell Tulsi not to worry."

But her confidence reeked of bullshit. Dad was in a bad way. I was no longer thinking about making it to the top. That had clearly been a pipe dream from the get-go. Now I was just wondering if we would make it through today—if we should continue the trek at all or just pack it in here and now. It would be a gigantic letdown for our fathers, but at this point their egos were nothing compared to their health. If we were to continue and something happened farther along the trail where it was impossible to get to a hospital . . .

"We don't have to do this," I whispered to Dad. "Nobody's going to judge you if we turn around. We can spend the two weeks sightseeing around Kathmandu—" He caught me with an icy glare, and I faltered for a moment before changing tactics. "Or if you're worried that you're holding us back from something—which you're not, we don't mind!—Sara and I will head to the top and we'll meet you and Albert afterward—"

"We're all heading to the top," he growled, wiping his brow and pulling himself to his feet. "With all due respect, Daughter, it is not your place to tell me what I can and cannot do. You are neither my doctor nor my wife. Now, stop nagging and let's ju-jube, or whatever the hell it is he keeps saying."

And with that, Dad ignited a ferocious resolve in both himself and Albert that I never expected in our mild-mannered fathers. Not that he suddenly *dashed* up those stairs—he took them gradually and deliberately, stopping every flight for a rest while Sara,

Albert, and I made small talk. Eventually, after three grueling hours, we made it to the top. Dad immediately sought solace under the shade of a tree, and I was relieved to see him grinning. As Sara busied herself refilling and purifying our water, Albert and I looked around.

We had arrived at a teahouse, the first of many tottering domiciles that would become our only deliverance from the unrelenting mountain trails. Teahouses are extremely modest inns built by the villagers where weary trekkers stop for meals or for the night. As the road we'd left was "the" road (the townships ahead would be accessible only by foot), all the materials had to be carried in on the backs of porters. We would soon discover that this made for dwellings that became increasingly creative the higher we went, but this first one was structurally sound, if basic.

Nearby was an outlook with a stunning view. I could barely make out the road we'd driven in on—a thin line ribboning next to a steel-colored river between two sharp hills. Buddhist prayer flags in yellow, green, red, white, and blue were strung crisscrossed in the trees just above our heads. After nearly an hour spent resting, eating momos, and drinking chai, Dad made a triumphant recovery. He was the first one to his feet when Bishwa gave the green light: "Jum-jum!"

"Let me hit the bathroom first," I said. "Bishwa, where is it?"

He responded with a blank stare.

"Uh . . . washroom? Lavatory? Water closet?" I paused for a minute, and then grabbed my crotch and hopped from one foot to the other in an embarrassing rendition of what I hoped was the international pee dance.

"Ah, toilet!" He laughed and pointed around the side of the building.

"*Dhanyabad.*" Sara used the Nepalese word for "thank you." "I have to go too."

We walked around the side of the building and found a rough-wood shack with a corrugated tin roof slightly shorter than we were. Pulling open the door revealed a hole, a pipe trickling water into a bucket, a wastebasket . . . and nothing more.

"You first," said Sara, handing me a packet of tissues.

I stepped inside and was nearly bowled over by the stench coming from the wastebasket. Apparently Dad wasn't the only trekker who'd eaten the cucumber. I closed the door—plunging myself into total darkness—and took a guess as to where the hole was. After tossing the tissue into the basket and flushing with the bucket, I burst out into the sunshine, gasping for air amid a swarm of shit-seeking flies.

"That was no toilet," I said. "That was a glorified hole. In fact, it wasn't even all that glorified."

"Antibac?" Sara squirted a drop from her little bottle into my hands. "You, ah, missed the hole, by the way."

I looked down to see a prominent sprinkle near the calf of my jeans. "Dammit!" Then I thought of something. "You know, Dad has bad knees and can't squat. How the hell is he going to—"

"Don't ask questions you don't want answers to." Sara shuddered. "And don't ever use the bathroom after him."

The afternoon went much better than the morning—namely because, while we did encounter a couple of staircases, none were as epic as the first. Instead, our path meandered along terraced fields near cottages where farmers toiled among clucking chickens and bouncing dogs. Little girls with long hair and nose rings hid shyly from us while the more raucous boys shouted "Hello!" or "*Namaste!*" The adults smiled and waved, evidently used to slack-jawed city slickers tromping clumsily through their backyards.

The villages were divided by long stretches of woodland. In the hollows of trees white orchids blossomed, their roots dangling in nappy tendrils. At one point, the trees gave way and we discovered that we were walking along the side of a deep valley. It was so large that we could barely make out the houses dotting the other side. We were transfixed by the view until the evening's chill filled the gorge with low-lying clouds so that nothing was visible but the creeping white mist.

Eventually we reached Pothana, which was our stop for the night. Just as we arrived, the looming clouds rumbled and ruptured. Raindrops clattered on the tin roofs like cutlery falling down the stairs, and we scrambled for shelter inside the teahouse. Dinner took place around a communal table in a dining area prematurely darkened by the inky sky. There was no power so we sat by candle-light—Sara and Dad chattering about everything we'd seen that day, Albert engaging Bishwa in simple conversation, and me writing about all of it in my journal—while we waited for our *dal bhat*.

"He said we were supposed to go twice as far today," said Albert when the meal arrived and Bishwa excused himself to eat with the other guides and porters.

"Yeah, it was the stairs that killed us," said Dad. "Sorry about that."

Albert waved his hand. "Don't be. Although apparently most people do them in about forty-five minutes."

"You're kidding. How long does it take the porters?"

"You don't want to know."

"I think we need to re-evaluate our trekking route." Sara spoke tenderly, but her words still stung with defeat. "There's no way we're going to make it to Base Camp. We overestimated our capabilities."

"We underestimated the challenge," interrupted Dad.

"Either way, we need a new plan. Any suggestions?"

I winced as I imagined how deflated our fathers must have felt. But, much to my surprise, they remained composed and pragmatic. Obviously we all had been thinking the same thing during those silent moments on the trail. And it wasn't as though we were giving up completely. Dad had made that very clear back on the stairs.

"It's difficult to gauge, because we're clearly not very good at predicting what lies in store or how we're going to handle it," said Albert.

"Since our trip is fourteen days, I say we just walk for a week and then turn around," suggested Dad. "Seven days in, seven days out."

In the end, we decided to take it day by day. Albert was right—there was no sense in drawing out a new plan if we didn't know what to expect. Chilly in our sweat-dampened clothing, it wasn't long after dinner that we said our good nights and hit the hay.

"So, what do you think?" asked Sara as we pulled out our sleeping bags.

"I think the people next to us should turn off their light. The bamboo weave in these walls is so thin that I could probably read right now. Also, have you seen the size of the gap under the door? Forget spiders—I'm worried that a cat's going to run in."

"I meant about the trek."

"Oh. Well, I think you lied about what a trek was." I crawled into bed. "But it actually wasn't *too* bad. Other than Dad almost dying, of course. It's sad that we won't be able to get to the top, but I'm sure we'll have fun anyway."

"Yeah. To be honest, my father told me before we left that he knew he wasn't going to make it all the way, so he's not disappointed. He's so happy he's here that he doesn't care how far we get. And I'm sure tomorrow will be better."

"Couldn't be much worse, right?" I said, unsure if I was kidding or not.

WE WERE UP early the next day, our muscles stiff but our spirits bright. The trek led us deeper into the rural hills. Villages became smaller and farther apart, while the forest grew lush. Spongy moss carpeted the rocks beneath the thick canopy overhead. Bamboo shoots grew in clusters thirty feet tall, their furry tops curving like the antennae of giant beetles. Massive trees with blossoms the size of baseballs loomed above us, their pink and red petals occasionally fluttering down onto our heads.

"Holy rhododendron, Batman," whistled Dad.

Our path grew onerous with breath-robbing inclines and crab-walking descents. We hiked on between rock-walled gorges where overgrowth hung high above us and finger waterfalls trickled down toward the river below. The shade was cool, almost worthy of a sweatshirt, but the beating sun was relentless.

Finally, we stopped for lunch. Sick of momos, we decided to try the noodle soup, and it came quickly—astonishingly quickly, in fact. Meals generally took at least forty-five minutes to arrive, as they often had to be cooked one by one. Not that it mattered, since we appreciated the excuse to sit the hell down. At least, Dad, Albert, and I did. Sara appeared to have a boundless supply of vigor as if she'd been storing it up for months like an energy-hoarding camel. Either that or she was secretly on speed. Whichever the case, I wished she'd share.

But anyway, back to the soup. In retrospect, we should've been more suspicious of how fast it had been cooked—especially since it was crucial that all our food have the bejesus boiled out of it. And by bejesus I mean the bacteria that the locals were immune to, but that would wreak havoc on our pampered Canadian systems. However, I didn't think anything of it until a couple of hours later when I started to feel a bit . . . iffy.

It began with fatigue. And not the perpetual yet manageable weariness associated with two days of hardcore walking. This was a sudden, crushing exhaustion that made me want to curl up on the path and take a nap. I was getting light-headed, and my stomach churned as if the noodles had sprung to life and were writhing within me like a nest of angry snakes. Needless to say, I was not at my zippiest.

"Jum-jum!" called Sara from up ahead where the rest of TAJ was waiting for me. "You're lagging!"

"Sorry," I grunted, pressing to catch up.

The hours wore on and my body wore down. At long last, we reached a village that Albert explained had once been called No Bridge but was recently renamed New Bridge due to the addition of a rickety suspension bridge that stretched across the boulder-studded river. The planks were set just slightly farther apart than the average human step, and the structure jerked beneath our weight. But the bridge was a cakewalk compared to what awaited us on the other side—another staircase as menacing as the first, stretching up into an abyss that may as well have been Guam for how far away it seemed to me.

Sara, of course, skipped all the way up. Albert was slow and steady, his wheezing no match for his determination. Dad surprised everybody when he tackled it like an expert, step by step with mindful intention—a triumphant comeback from his ass whooping of yesterday. But I was floundering. After just a few stairs, I had to sit down and will my lunch back to its rightful position. My body felt heavy and broken. Eventually, I resorted to crawling on all fours.

"Daughter, what's up with you?" Dad yelled when I yet again sank into the stairs for a rest, the cold stone seeming to twist and squirm beneath me. "We're like fifty feet from dinner!"

"I'm not feeling well," I replied meekly.

"Well, you can be sick once we get there. Now stop whining and let's go!"

Gritting my teeth, I continued my scramble upward. I was torn between embarrassment at being the weakest link and resentment at Dad's lack of empathy—and after I showed nothing but compassion when he nearly had a cardiac arrest on a similar set of steps yesterday! But after what felt like an eternity, I crested the top and staggered into New Bridge. While the rest of TAJ beelined for the dining area of the teahouse, I went to lie down.

"Wow, you're actually *that* overtired?" asked Sara. "You are *really* not used to exercise!"

I mustered just enough strength to glare at her before collapsing into bed. When I awoke two hours later, things had gone from bad to worse.

"Sara! Bucket!" I cried, flinging back the sheets. "Bucketbucket bucketbuck—*blegh*!"

And so began what would be known from that day forth as Black Noodle Soup Thursday. I don't know if it actually *was* a Thursday, but that's hardly relevant. I can honestly say that it wasn't until I was puking my guts out in a teahouse with the architectural stability of a Jenga game that I felt like a true backpacker. And, by that definition, Sara, Dad, and Albert were also about to achieve true backpacker status by participating in what was the most epic cookie toss off I had ever encountered.

But I'm getting ahead of myself. Back to the bedroom, where Sara had just managed to shove the wastebasket under my nose in the nick of time.

"Ugghh," I groaned. "Gross."

Dad knocked on the door and asked what the commotion was about. When he saw the state I was in, he immediately designated himself as hair-holder, water-fetcher, and wastebasket-emptier while I sat there whimpering and feeling sorry for myself.

"I don't know what you ate," he said as he handed me a tissue to wipe my face. "But I'm glad I didn't have any."

A rumble in my southern regions suggested that this wasn't going to be just a bucket job. "Uh-oh. I have to go to the bathroom. Can you give me a hand?"

"Sure thing, Daughter." He stood up and extended his arm for me to lean on as I crawled weakly out of bed. Three steps toward the door, however, and my knees gave way as the noodles once again wrought their vengeance on my upper digestive tract.

"Oh god—whenever I walk, I barf." This was becoming a catastrophe.

Without a word, Dad scooped me up in his arms. Kicking open the door, he stepped out into the night where the temperature had dropped and our breath hung in the air like comic book speech bubbles. And when I was done in the toilet shack, Dad was right there ready to carry me back to bed. Resting my head against his chest, the animosity I'd felt toward him earlier disappeared. Now, I was overwhelmed with love for the man who was just as eager to trek Nepal with his daughter as he was to lug her sick ass to the can.

When we got back to the room, we discovered that Sara had also started to feel . . . iffy. Her face had gone the same funny color as when we were on the shark boat, and it wasn't long before she too was making acquaintance with the wastebasket—her body convulsing as Dad held her hair out of the way.

"Now who's overtired?" I muttered, though quietly enough that she wouldn't hear.

With two quivering messes now in his charge, Dad set up camp on our bedroom floor. Bishwa and the porters brought us boiled water and sat vigil in the room next door, their light burning long after the other guides had gone to sleep. Of course, as if by clockwork, just when Sara finally got it all out of her system, it was Dad's turn.

"Goddamn noodle soup," he gasped as he dove for the bucket. What a night.

The next morning I awoke feeling tired but stable. Sara and Dad were still asleep, so I gathered my journal and slipped out the door to go write at the picnic table outside. I was just about to sit down when I caught my first glimpse of a mountain peak—pale blue and capped with snow beyond a plait of overlapping foothills. That was it. That was what we were working toward. Awestruck and placated, I sat down to admire the view just as Albert appeared with two steaming cups of chai.

"You all had a bit of a rough night, I take it?" he said as he sat down.

"There's an understatement."

"Alas, I did as well."

"So, have you seen it yet?"

"Seen what?"

I gestured past him and he turned around, his face breaking into a smile as he laid eyes upon the mountain. "It's funny, isn't it?" he said. "We spend all night in the clutches of agony, and yet we wake up to such a sublime sight that everything seems all right somehow."

"Nepal is a crazy place. I can't decide if I love it or hate it."

Albert laughed. "That sounds about right from what I remember forty years ago. But it's these complex places that earn a spot in your heart. Now, let's have some tea. Goodness knows we need it."

BLACK NOODLE SOUP Thursday was followed by Recovery Friday, which was spent lying around and drinking fluids. A couple of other trekkers stopped at the teahouse for lunch, and as we talked with them I realized how much of an anomaly we were. They were mostly in their thirties—wiry Europeans with the latest gear and calf muscles like potatoes. Many of them had done the Alps (or the Andes, or Kilimanjaro), and all were avid hikers. They seemed bemused to meet us but were warmed by our ragtaggery and wished us the best on the trail.

The next day, with our jaws set and our hearts respunked, we hit the road. And by road, I mean stairs. Holy crap, do I mean stairs.

They were literally just flattened rocks crammed into the hillside—jagged, uneven, and so tall that I was starting to suspect that Nepalis were born without torsos and instead went right from neck to leg. It was the only explanation for how they were able to take such gigantic steps. And these stairs went on *forever*. Up and up and up . . . Here in this dizzyingly thin-aired world, up was not so much a direction as it was a philosophy, a way of life, or, in our case, a four-letter word. Whenever we encountered a fork in the trail, the direction we were to head was always up.

"If we go up any farther, we'll enter orbit," grumbled Dad.

And even on the rare occasions when we were able to go down (on a bone-jarringly, stomach-wrenchingly steep plane), the joy of the experience was tarnished with the law of the mountains: what goes down, must come up—and probably twice as far. Our first question to Bishwa each morning was where we would have lunch, and he would point at a teahouse close enough that we could make out the color of its roof. However, we would be gazing across a valley—which meant we'd have to spend hours going *aaaaaallllllll* the way down to the bottom only to hop across a stream and then come *aaaaallllllll* the way back up again. Bridge builders could have lucrative careers in the Annapurnas.

My legs burned, my lungs burned, my bowels burned with the scrappy remains of the Black Noodle Soup bacteria. My heart sputtered and made the same clunking noise that my mother's car did before conking out on the highway. The teahouses began to resemble structures painted by Salvador Dalí, with slippery perspectives and corners that didn't quite meet at right angles. Likewise, the food grew increasingly surreal—"pizza" was anything from flatbread with ketchup to tomato soup served with slice-shaped triangles drawn on top with cream.

"I love dessert," said Albert when we happened upon the

luxury of instant custard. "It really gets the taste of supper out of your mouth."

We caught occasional glimpses of the mountain, ghostly in the midday haze—a massive dangling carrot reminding us what we were sweating for. We passed shrines adorned with painted Buddha eyes and flapping prayer flags, some of which housed mountainside cemeteries with photos of the dead and bouquets of flowers. It really was beautiful. However, I was having a difficult time appreciating it as my lungs screamed in agony. Sensing my distress, Sara brought out the secret weapon that she'd kept hidden until the perfect moment.

"Susunka," she said, using the pet name bestowed upon me by my Polish grandmother. "If you make it to that next ridge, I'll give you a pink Mentos."

"You have *Mentos*?" I cried, suddenly forgetting the misery of my plight. "And you've been holding out on me *all this time*?"

"Not holding out. Saving. They're *all* pink, too. And you get to have one as soon as we get to the top of the next hill."

Sometimes dangling carrots aren't incentive enough for me. Candy, on the other hand, works every time. Unfortunately, not everyone was as easily pacified. Mentos couldn't have done anything to relieve poor Albert's grief. He doubled over with coughs so violent I worried they would send him over the side of the mountain. But he never griped about it. In fact, he even went so far as to apologize for holding us up. I was beginning to understand Sara's fortitude more and more.

At long last, we arrived in Chhomrong. It is the hub where many treks intersect, so the teahouses were a little less sketchy. While Bishwa signed us in, Dad excused himself to visit the bathroom. When he returned, he had the biggest grin I'd seen on his face since the day we arrived in Kathmandu. "It's a Western toilet!" he cried. "And they have *showers*!"

Okay, I'll admit it. Yes, this was the first shower I'd taken since Pokhara. And yes, I smelled like a ferret. My newly acquired musk was an offensive blend of dirt and old sweat, exacerbated by a limited supply of T-shirts and only one pair of pants. The water was freezing and my bar of soap spent most of its time squirming around the concrete floor, but that didn't matter. When I emerged, I felt refreshed and invigorated—the memory of Black Noodle Thursday finally banished to a back corner of my mind.

Over dinner, we turned again to a discussion of our plan. Just like the last time, our conclusion was bittersweet.

"Bishwa says we might be able to make Base Camp after all," said Sara. "We did surprisingly well today. It's six days up and back from here."

Albert sighed. "You'll have to do it without me," he said. "I just don't have the puff. I'll wait here for your return."

"Dad, are you sure? The Bedfords can go—I'll stay here with you!"

He waved his hand. "Nonsense. This is what you're here for, kiddo. I had my chance. When you come back to Nepal with your child in forty years, then you can stay behind. But now, go see that mountain."

Sara hugged him, teary-eyed. Dad and I exchanged a sad smile across the table.

The next morning, we bid our farewells to Albert and set off. Bishwa walked beside me as he had discovered what Dad and Sara already knew: that I possessed all the grace of a snowplow. My feet acted as though they were completely unacquainted and this resulted in several stumbles accompanied with a high-pitched "*Waa!*" It wasn't a big deal on flatter terrain, but on the steep stairs—especially those that vanished into oblivion on one side—it was a serious concern. And so Bishwa had assigned himself to Sue duty, ready to save me in case I fell off the edge of the world.

Dad and Sara, meanwhile, began a daily tally of my gravitational misgivings.

"*Waa!*"

"Five," Dad and Sara said in unison. The porters giggled.

We were often passed along the trail by locals carrying food and supplies. Sometimes they were transporting ridiculously cumbersome items like propane tanks or bricks—yet they always traveled in flip-flops at the same brisk pace. Once, after I'd just clambered up a particularly unforgiving staircase and was feeling quite proud of myself, I was asked to move aside for a fourteen-year-old girl with a mini fridge strapped to her back.

"I don't care what those gym rats press," said Sara as she stared in disbelief. "Nobody is as fit as a Nepalese porter."

We spent the night in the hamlet of Bamboo—aptly located within a thick bamboo forest—and it took me over an hour to fall asleep because it was absolutely *freezing*. When I went for my midnight bathroom run (bats whizzing above me), the pee actually steamed. I couldn't believe I was fighting my two worst enemies—cold and exercise—on top of a mountain. My life had officially become a Japanese cartoon.

Up'ing out of the bamboo of Bamboo, I was shocked to see how fast the ecosystem changed with the altitude. Suddenly, the trees had almost no leaves and the grass was yellow and dead. Lumps of wet snow collected in the streams. The waterfalls were at their finest, cascading down like tinsel on a Christmas tree. Right after lunch, the clouds rolled in—and less than an hour later, it started to pour. By the time we arrived breathless and shivering in Deurali, the hail was pounding the roofs like gunfire. Icicles began to form with incredible speed, growing an inch every thirty minutes.

After dinner, we huddled around the table with our hats on our heads and our hands on our chai, and swapped stories with the other travelers.

"Oh, *you're* the family of four who got sick from the noodle soup!" cried a woman from New Zealand. "I've heard about you! Your story is spreading along the trail."

"Look at that, I've become famous for puking!" Dad shook his head incredulously. "That fortune cookie was *way* off."

By morning, the ground was covered in a thin sheet of ice. I dressed inside my sleeping bag—two pairs of socks, long johns, jeans, a T-shirt, a turtleneck, a raincoat, a puffy vest, a hat, thin gloves, and mittens. But despite my being swaddled up like a papoose, the biting cold still penetrated my muscles, which were wound tight from days of overuse. The pain was sharp and I thought for sure that something would snap—rendering me jellified and sobbing in the middle of nowhere.

Trying to walk on the ice was difficult to the point of ridiculousness. Had we a couple of cream pies and a slide whistle we could've passed for the Three Stooges. My jeans were soon streaked with slush and I discovered that my hiking boots were waterproof in name only. By that point, we were almost completely beyond the tree line (with the exception of the occasional rhododendron—fuchsia blossoms covered in ice crystals); all that lay before us was brown rock patched with snow and countless silver waterfalls.

In those early-morning hours, I was not a tickled trekker. But when the sun finally burst over the peaks and bathed the valley in light, my mood lifted. Suddenly, I was smitten with the weird beauty and extreme remoteness. As we skipped from stone to stone across a bubbling river, I realized we were no longer heading *toward* the mountains—we were *in* the mountains. The Himalayas had snuck up on us when we weren't paying attention, now rising on all sides to mind-boggling heights. In the distance, there was a low rumble as an avalanche hurtled enormous chunks of snow and ice down the cliff.

"This is . . . I don't even know what to say." Sara shook her head. "It's got to be the most beautiful place on earth."

"I can't imagine anything more perfect," Dad agreed. "And just think, by this afternoon, we'll be at the top. Next is Machhapuchhre Base Camp for lunch, and then ABC. We're almost there—nothing can stop us!"

Of course, not two hours later, something stopped us.

Just as they had the day before, the clouds encroached dark and sinister. Slush began to fall, freezing our jackets in crispy layers that crackled like firewood as we struggled forth. With the stroke of luck that had remained with us since Pothara, we arrived at the teahouse minutes before the blizzard tore through the mountains with a frightening rage. The snow whipped and whirled in frenzied gales while thunder rattled the windows and lightning split the sky with purple-white forks. It was like two storms at once—one arctic and one electric. And while I didn't believe in anything supernatural, I had to admit that between the weather and the mountains it did feel as though there was some sort of terrible divinity surging and crashing around us.

Heavenly arena or not, one thing was clear: there was no way we were making it to ABC that afternoon. And so, with our damp socks drying by the heater, we hunkered down as the storm bore late into the night. Although I stole all the blankets from the empty rooms, I still lay sleepless for hours, kept awake by the sound of my own chattering teeth.

"Susunka," a voice whispered in the dark just as I was beginning to doze off. "Jum-jum."

"It's like midnight, Sara. Go back to sleep."

"Actually, it's five thirty in the morning."

"I refer you to the previous statement."

"Come on, get up! It's ABC time!"

I groaned and pulled the blanket over my head as she started singing the alphabet song. How could anybody be this chipper while it was still dark outside? I knew I must've slept at some point, but I was still exhausted. Even though this was the day we'd been waiting for, I wasn't very excited. In fact, all I wanted to do was curl up like a hedgehog and slip into hibernation.

Somehow, Sara and Dad managed to drag me out of bed and into the dining area. They squealed and tittered while I sulked into my oatmeal. We hadn't even left the teahouse and already my fingers and toes were stinging frostily.

"Good?" Bishwa gave me the thumbs-up sign.

Grumpy, I shook my head and rubbed my arms. "Cold."

"Ah, yes. They cold too." He pointed to the porters. They were pulling plastic bags over their flip-flops and tying them to their ankles with blue twine. "Winter boots," he explained.

Wonderful—now I can't even complain anymore, I thought. *Thanks a lot, Bishwa.*

Outside, the world was enveloped in a gray predawn light, and I felt like I was part of a charcoal sketch. On the ground lay five inches of snow, pristine save for the footsteps of the two or three trekkers who had set out even earlier that morning. A stillness hung around us—a quiet so tangible it was like the air had been stuffed with cotton. Had it not been for the crunch of our shoes on the snow, I would've thought that I had gone deaf in the night.

"Well," Dad whispered so as not to break the atmosphere. "I'll be honest with you: there was a time I truly didn't think we'd make it. Yet here we are in the home stretch. Now we just have to take that last giant leap for Team Average Joe . . . I'll see you at the top."

"Woo!" cried Sara, clapping her mittened hands. "Let's do this!"

And with that, we set out on the final leg toward Annapurna Base Camp.

THUS BEGAN ONE of the most treacherous days of my life. The air was so cold that breathing it was like inhaling razor blades. I had lost all sensation in my toes and wondered if they were still attached to my feet or had splintered off to rattle around in my boots like loose pebbles. I would have burst into tears if I hadn't been so afraid that they'd freeze over my eyeballs, trapping me in a frosted world of ice and pain. Who was I kidding? I was no trekker, and I was certainly not one for this frozen hell. I got cold reaching into the freezer for peas! What had ever possessed me to do this in the first place?

I halted in my tracks, arms crossed, lip drooping. That was it. I was done. They could go to ABC. I was just going to stand right here and wait for them to return.

"Daughter," Dad lumbered back down the path toward me. "What's wrong?"

"I'm cold and I'm tired and I want to go home!" I knew I sounded an eight-year-old, but I didn't care anymore. The mountain had beaten me. It had crushed my gentle spirit and soaked my expensive hiking boots. *You win, Annapurna Base Camp. I give up.*

I expected Dad to roll his eyes and make some snarky quip, but he didn't. Instead, he took off his sunglasses and looked at me with that warm, patient expression that comes with two decades of experience being a father.

"Susan," he said in a voice that was both soft and stern. "I know this isn't your idea of a party. But look how far you've come. You deserve to make it to the top. You've worked for it, sweated for it, froze for it, and puked for it. So get up there. And do it not only for yourself, but for all the wimpy, deadbeat, pipe-dreaming Average Joes out there."

It was the most double-edged pep talk I'd ever received, but it did the trick. Slowly, and still sporting a level-five pout, I trudged up the trail until finally I reached the teahouse where Sara was waiting.

"We're here! We're at Annapurna Base Camp!" she shrieked.

And so we were. The Himalayas surrounded us as if we were inside a bowl. From where we stood, we could see the peaks of Annapurna One, Annapurna Three, Machhapuchhre, and Annapurna South. Never had I been in the presence of anything so epic. It was a rushing sensation of reverse vertigo in both a physical and philosophical way. I was suddenly overwhelmed by the feeling of our utmost inconsequentiality as we were nearly dwarfed out of existence by the mighty mountains.

Of course, had I said any of those things, it would have made for a more treasured moment. Instead, I blurted out: "Whoa! It looks like the Coors Light beer can!"

Sara raised one eyebrow. "And you're a writer, huh?"

Twenty minutes later, we were making our victory official with a celebratory Fanta when the tranquility was interrupted by what sounded like a swarm of eggbeaters descending from the heavens. We watched aghast as a private helicopter landed twenty yards from where we sat. The door opened and a well-dressed Arab couple in their mid-thirties stepped out. They stood in the snow for a few minutes, snapped a few pictures, then climbed back on board their chopper and took off once more.

"What the heck was that?" asked Sara.

"*That* was a couple of pansies," scoffed Dad. Cupping his hands, he yelled at the helicopter, "We trekked the whole thing, you losers!"

"You *princesses*!" I shouted, grinning.

It may have been a party at the top, but the way back down was serious business. If we wanted to reach Chhomrong by the next evening, we would have to cover a lot of ground. The midday sun was quickly melting the new-fallen snow, and it wasn't long before the mountain turned into one great big slip-and-slide.

Even Bishwa was wiping out. At one point, I fell and skidded for fifteen feet before coming to a rest—streaked with dirt from hood to ankle—in front of a family of six.

"*Safe!*" yelled the father.

"Heh, good one," chuckled Dad.

The snow turned to slush turned to mud; the rocks turned to tundra turned to forest. We copied the porters and put plastic bags on our feet, using them as an extra layer between our socks and our shoes. Our faces, meanwhile, grew quite sunburned—Sara's sunglasses had given her reverse raccoon eyes, and I looked like I'd spontaneously developed vitiligo. Outside Bamboo, Bishwa hacked down walking sticks for us, which improved not only our physical comfort, but also our wanderlust image. Needless to say, I couldn't imagine what Albert thought of us when we finally rocked up to Chhomrong.

"Welcome back!" he said as he pulled Sara into a tight hug. "I'm so glad you made it. Showers are down the hall on the left. We'll talk after."

And so the most challenging part of the trek was complete. As we descended, the landscape flourished. Some areas were nothing but rhododendrons—candy-floss woodlands stretching as far as the eye could see—and others were forests, shadowed in the deeper caverns of the gorge where a spooky mist hung around our ankles. As the days grew warmer, I donned fewer grubby layers until I was down to the jeans and T-shirt I'd started in. The villages grew larger and closer together, and as the trekking season entered full swing they bustled with travelers following the route in the other direction. Then, one afternoon—in a quiet moment of modesty and anticlimax—we stumbled out of the woods and onto the road.

"Finish!" said Bishwa as the porters clapped.

"That's it?" asked Dad. "We're done? Just like that?"

"Don't tell me you want to go again," said Albert.

"No, I just . . ." he looked around. "I can't believe it's over. What a weird two weeks."

As we settled into our last teahouse before the ride back to Pokhara, I did something I hadn't dared to do while on the trail: I looked in the mirror. What stared back at me was not the person I expected—the fresh-faced, bright-eyed girl that was frequently asked out on dates. No, this person was *hideous*. My skin was a calico blend of browns and pinks amid newly hatched freckles and streaks of dirt. My lips were chapped and my nose was raw from being wiped in the cold air. My shoelaces emitted a mushroom cloud of dust when I untied them, and I was pretty sure my jeans could stand up under their own free will.

"Sweet Moses!" I recoiled from my reflection in horror. "I look like my passport photo fell down a cliff!"

"Nah," said Sara as she stepped out of the shower with a towel around her head. "You just look like a trekker, that's all."

When we returned to Kathmandu, we discovered that Tulsi had arranged a dinner for us. As we sat around the restaurant with festive dots of colored ash on our foreheads and plates heaped high with steaming treats, we regaled him with the tribulations of the trek—which suddenly seemed hilarious now that we were warm and sitting down.

"I lost fifteen pounds these last two weeks," boasted Dad as he helped himself to a second round of momos. "I'm sure I'll find it again soon, but in the meantime I need a new belt."

Tulsi laughed and shook his head. "When you came into my office that day . . . you were one of the most unprepared groups I'd ever met. Bishwa called me on that first afternoon and said that there was *no way* you'd ever make it. So, it's with a genuine heart that I congratulate you."

"To Team Average Joe!" cried Sara.

"Who's Joe?" asked Tulsi. "Anyway, this calls for a celebration! Should I order some drinks? Nepalese liquor?"

"Thank you, but no," said Albert. "Just chai, please."

The rest of us nodded in agreement. After all, there would be plenty of time for alcohol when we ditched our parents again.

- 3 -

Not-So-Holier Than Thou

Me: *Does this rice have yak in it?*
Amaya: *Everything has yak in it.*
Me: *What doesn't have yak in it?*
Amaya: *The rice, once you pick the yak out.*

APRIL SEVENTEENTH BROUGHT with it a warm breeze, the acrid smell of distant fires, and my twenty-fourth birthday. I was nearly a quarter of a century old. At this age, Alexander the Great invaded Persia and Kurt Cobain wrote *Nevermind*. Yet here I was with no job, no degree, no apartment, and no boyfriend. On the bright side, I was about to cross from Kathmandu into Tibet. It wasn't quite as impressive as seizing Asia Minor, but it would do for now.

As it was illegal for travelers to venture unaccompanied through the country, we signed up for a tour. But when our tuk-tuk dropped us off at the designated meeting spot (which turned out to be a weedy, oil-stained parking lot), we discovered that things were a little . . . disorganized. A large bus idled across five parking spaces, the luggage hatches sprang open like beetle wings. Backpackers stood around yawning and smoking while two Tibetan men scurried between them waving bundles of crinkled documents.

"Excuse me!" called Sara, flagging down the nearest Tibetan. "Hello! We're here for the trip. My name is—"

"Okayokay," the man nodded impatiently. He shuffled through his papers and thrust a poorly photocopied page at each of us. "Yes here now."

"Uh . . ." I glanced down at what looked to be a schedule of the excursion. "I'm guessing this means we're in the right place . . . ?"

"I'm not sure he speaks English," said Sara. "Maybe we should talk to the other guy."

"Neither of them speak English—they just arrange English words into arbitrary patterns." A brown-skinned girl with a shaved head appeared at my elbow and compared her schedule to mine. "Hmm, my itinerary doesn't list any of the same places that yours does."

"Mine's dated from three years ago," said an Australian woman wearing yoga pants.

"Mine lists somebody named 'Susan Bedford' as the tour operator," said a Vietnamese guy with glasses, and a few others nodded in agreement.

I grabbed his paper. "What the? *I'm* Susan Bedford! Why is my name on there?"

"Guess you're the special one." The Vietnamese guy shrugged. "Must be your birthday or something."

I looked up sharply as Sara guffawed. We were off to a weird start.

After a seven-hour border crossing (during which all guidebooks referencing Tibet as an independent state were seized), we piled into the bus and began crawling up dizzyingly sheer foothills. When I looked across the valley, I could see separate villages staggered vertically along the mountainside like glittering trinkets on a stack of shelves. Meanwhile, the road twisted and writhed in turns so perilous that the bus often had to take up both of the narrow lanes. Looking out the window, I couldn't even see the ledge below us. Our tires were rolling along the edge of the abyss.

The land soon became too steep for development, and the thick carpet of pine trees surrounded us on all sides, unbroken except for the serpentine road. The low-hanging clouds hid the top of the hills and mist soon blanketed the bottom. As both twilight and a light rain began to fall, I was struck by the strange sensation that we were traveling not between countries but between planes of existence. Eventually, the temperature dropped enough that the windows fogged over, and the gossamer universe beyond faded into white.

The next day, we arrived at the roof of the world.

If this fraction of Asia was a house and Kathmandu its kitchen—smoky, bustling, vibrant with scent and spice—then we had spent the evening creeping up rickety staircases and forgotten mezzanines before slipping through a trapdoor onto a mysterious plateau of bright desolation. We were far above the reaches of foliage. The landscape, parched and cold, was pale with steel mountaintops peeking over the horizon. There was an aura here—so isolated, so esoteric—that made me believe we could hide away forever without being discovered.

"This place is tripping me out," I said.

"Actually, it's the altitude that's tripping you out," said Sara, and I noticed her voice had acquired a dribbly drawl. "That last pass was over 16,000 feet. Our brains are a little oxygen deprived right now."

"Is that what that is?" Ever since we'd left Nepal, I had been feeling increasingly mellow and fuzzy. But it wasn't unpleasant. In fact, it made ten hours on a bus seem not so bad.

Occasionally, our two-lane highway passed beneath an archway strung with over a thousand Tibetan prayer flags that fluttered noisily like a flock of starlings. Yaks pulled antiquated plows in barren fields and woolly sheep skittered across the road. Farmers with faces burnt from sun and wind swung lassos while women fussed over children who looked like little Ewoks in yak-fur coats and hats.

"It's amazing, isn't it?" said the girl with the shaved head, whose name was Amaya. "This place is so surreal. It makes me feel like I'm in a dream."

"I thought the same thing, but my friend says it's just oxygen deprivation," I replied.

She laughed. "Perhaps. So, how long are you two in Asia for?"

"Probably for the rest of the year," said Sara. She explained our trip.

"Cool. What do you do back home?"

"I'm a nurse."

"A nurse!" Amaya was impressed. "That's an incredible job. You get to really make a difference. Not to mention the fact that there are so many opportunities to travel with it. Seriously, good for you."

"Thanks!" Sara beamed.

Amaya turned to me. "Are you also a nurse?"

"No no," I waved the notion away with my hand. "I'm a waitress."

"Oh. You must still be studying then."

"Nope."

"So you've graduated?"

The muscles in my jaw twitched. "Nope."

"Oh. Well . . ." she paused, thinking of something to say. "At least you've got lots of free time to travel."

It was a conversation I'd had a hundred times—rationally, I knew it wasn't a big deal. Nobody ever treated me differently than Sara when they learned our occupations. And even if, in some condemnatory corner of their minds, they thumbed their noses at the fact that I spiced their Caesars and rescued their fallen spoons, so what? It didn't matter because we were only crossing paths—ships in the night and all that.

No, what bothered me was that every time I had that discussion it reminded me that eventually I would have to return home to . . . what? I had no idea. Sara was so lucky. She had it all carved out. I, on the other hand, felt like that one lost sock in the dryer— spinning in circles until I was faded and sick.

This was so harshing my mellow.

Just then, the driver pulled over to the side of the road and yanked me from my woebegone thoughts. We parked next to a peculiar structure resembling a partially constructed hut on stilts.

"Pee-pee ka-ka!" called the guide. "Go-go!"

"What's he saying?" asked Sara as we stepped off the bus.

"I think he means it's a bathroom break, but I have no idea what that's got to do with—oh dear lord."

There was an older Chinese lady on the tour who evidently was familiar with the structure. She wasted no time in hauling herself up a ladder to a second-story platform where she squatted behind a half wall, hidden from sight. There were a few conspicuous sounds, and then a singular turd free-fell ten feet through the open air before landing with an icky plop on the ground below.

"Incoming!" yelled the Vietnamese guy as we reeled backward to avoid the splatter.

"Ew!" cried Sara. A piece of toilet paper fluttered down like a soiled butterfly. "What on earth . . . ?"

"You're next," I said.

She rolled her eyes. "As if. I'm going to go behind a rock. Like a *lady*."

I looked back up at the platform and shook my head. "And it just keeps getting weirder and weirder."

SHORTLY THEREAFTER, WE came across our first monastery. Nepal had been fairly religious (what with the deity statues in Kathmandu and the shrines in the countryside) but it didn't hold a yak-butter candle to the piety of Tibet. Here, Buddhism was the thread that stitched together the collective consciousness of everyday life. Many families still followed the tradition of sending their second son to become a monk at age seven; and since monastic life hadn't changed much in the last few hundred years, there was a strong connection between the monks of today and their religious forefathers.

In terms of the monastery, I had no idea what to expect. Most of the people I knew were somewhere between agnostic and atheist, except for my grandmother (deeply Catholic in that "old country" way) and my aunt (who put both the "fun" and the "mental" in fundamental Christian). But even their spiritual inclination didn't define their every moment. There were bibles to be thumped, of course, but also work to be done, money to be made, people and hobbies to be entertained. The fact that these monks' entire lives were devoted to, well, devotion . . . it blew my mind. I pictured a group of blissed-out bald guys levitating a couple of inches above their prayer mats.

"I don't think they *actually* levitate," said Sara as we neared the monastery.

"I don't know. I've heard it takes ten thousand hours to become a master at something, and surely these guys have spent more than that amount of time meditating. Hell, I bet some of them can do loop-de-loops by now!"

"Sue, Tibetan Buddhist monks achieve spiritual enlightenment through profound introspection and the elimination of desire. They do *not* do loop-de-loops."

I snorted. "Says you."

I had it in mind that the monastery would be modest. An empty room for thinking, or not thinking, or whatever it was that got a person "enlightened." Barren walls with good acoustics for chanting. Hopefully a better toilet system than the one we'd seen earlier. I couldn't speak for the monks, but I'd never be able to attain inner peace knowing that my every nugget would be whizzing through the air like an Olympic diver.

It turned out I was wrong about everything except the toilet system.

There were grandiose hallways and winding staircases, high-ceilinged chambers, and pocketed alcoves. The walls were painted with gigantic mandalas in glittering gold leaf, and the dusty shelves were filled with stacks of hallowed texts. Golden Buddhas encrusted with sapphires, emeralds, and rubies ranged from two to twenty feet in height, occupying every niche and nave. Out of the corner of my eye, I thought for sure I saw them twitch—but that was just an illusion cast by the flickering light of hundreds of candles. The air was musty, filled with shadow and an almost palpable silence. There were no monks to be seen.

"This place is intense," whispered Sara as we set off to explore. "It feels different in here. Tranquil yet vibrant. Like there's been some sort of shift in the energy." She took a deep breath, her eyes reflecting the dancing candlelight. "Just think about the thousands of monks who have spent hundreds of years meditating in here. I know you're a skeptic when it comes to this stuff, but can't you sense the residual . . . something?"

I closed my eyes and inhaled deeply, wondering for a wild, fanciful moment whether I too would feel the residual something glissading beyond my fingertips or whispering on the nape of my neck. Instead, however, I just felt my sinuses reacting to the dust.

As we wandered around, I tried to imagine what it'd be like to spend every day from childhood until death within these walls. It seemed like the antithesis of Western mentality, where life is measured by its anticipations, challenges, accomplishments, and failures. We were constantly preoccupied with either what we'd done or what we were going to do. But for a monk, a homogeneous lifestyle rendered such notions meaningless.

So what was a person who spent all day journeying to the darkest recesses of his soul actually *like*? What sort of mind developed when deprived of economical fluctuations and familial pressures and MTV? Surely these were solemn individuals who didn't waste their cerebral fortitude on the silliness that occupied ninety-nine-point-nine percent of our lay-brains. They probably concentrated their every waking moment on illumination and transcendence.

Just then, we turned a corner and happened upon our first real monk. We watched quietly, trying not to disturb him as he slid back and forth across the room in long, smooth strides, with what appeared to be rags tied to his slippers. His hands were clasped behind his back and he was whistling an upbeat tune.

"What's he doing?" I whispered to Sara. "Is he performing some sort of ancient Tibetan meditation ritual?"

"No," she whispered back. "I think . . . I think he's dusting the floor."

At that moment, the monk looked up, jumped with surprise, and nearly fell on his holy ass. His face turned the same scarlet as his robes as he shrugged sheepishly.

"Well," said Sara as we stifled our giggles and continued on our way. "I suppose he was just having a little fun."

"Are they, like, *allowed* to do that?" I wondered, although Sara had meandered ahead and didn't hear me.

FROM THERE ON in, it was hysteria-monasteria. They were everywhere—the Tibetan version of Starbucks. Each one housed a plethora of golden Buddhas, elaborate decorations, and monks who may not have been skating around the room but who weren't levitating, either. Many of them did seem to be involved in spiritual rituals, such as chanting or praying. But every now and again we'd catch one that was dozing off, or whispering to his neighbor, or doing something else that seemed suspiciously . . . human.

One afternoon, as Sara and I were trying to warm up in the sunshine, we noticed a group of young monks staring at us and chattering rapidly to one another. After what looked like quite the debate, one guy was thrust forward by his peers and stumbled toward us with a shy smile and an awkward teenage gait.

"Hello. I . . . like . . . your . . . hair!" he said in staggered English, referring to the dreadlocked tresses that hung down to my elbows.

"Thanks!" I beamed. Then, with the automatic reflexes of returning a compliment, added, "I like your hair too!"

The monk ran one hand over his shaved head and gave me a quizzical look.

The next day, we arrived in the city of Lhasa, which teemed with stark contrasts between Tibetan tradition and Chinese influence. Soldiers with machine guns watched from the rooftops while welders made repairs on the sidewalks with DIY masks of paper plates and sunglasses. Convenience stores were stocked with everything from candied breadsticks to corn-flavored ice cream, and pilgrims shopped for prayer wheels in Barkhor Square. Overlooking it all was Potala Palace—once the winter home of the Dalai Lama—so splashy and ostentatious that it made the Vatican look underdressed.

"I don't care what you say about altitude, this place *is* trippy," I said to Sara.

When we were given the afternoon to explore independently, Amaya, Sara, and I immediately headed to Barkhor Square. While most of Lhasa was Chinese (in an attempt to eradicate Tibetan culture, the government had encouraged people from the rest of China to settle there), Barkhor Square had remained fiercely true to its Tibetan heritage and was one of the most sacred spots for Buddhists.

"It's a lifelong dream for many Tibetans to make the pilgrimage here," explained Amaya. "But it isn't enough to just walk to Barkhor. Instead, they practice a ritual wherein after every single step they reach up to the sky, then touch their hands to their throats, then throw themselves to the ground and slide forward on their stomachs."

"Wait a sec," I interrupted. "They do that *all the way here*? Doesn't that take, like, *months* if they're coming from far away?"

Amaya nodded. "You got it. And once they arrive, they still have to circle the square clockwise one hundred and eight times before they're done."

"You're telling me these people slither like inchworms over frozen tundra for months on end, driven by nothing but spiritual compulsion? I have to see it to believe it."

Then I saw it and still didn't believe it. Men and women of all ages were hurling themselves at the ground and skidding forward like curling stones. Pads or small planks of wood were attached to their forearms and shins to decrease friction. Their clothing was filthy and torn, and on their foreheads were black scabs like cigar burns where the skin had been scraped away. They looked exhausted and in pain—yet eerily elated. I had never witnessed such determination in my life.

"Holy crap, that's brutal." I winced as I rubbed my own forehead.

"They don't call it religious sacrifice for nothing," said Amaya.

However, it seemed like not everybody was taking such an extreme approach. In fact, most people were just walking normally. After watching from the sidelines for a bit, Sara, Amaya, and I jumped in and joined the hundreds of pilgrims. They wore enormous fur hats and the Asian equivalent of mukluks. Many of them were chanting and carrying prayer wheels, which were silver barrels containing prayer scrolls spinning on the end of short sticks. More than once I felt a tug on my dreadlocks and then turned around to find a handful of people examining my hair—one lady even sniffed a lock, then hopped backward in disgust.

That night, the three of us headed to a tea shop. We had originally ventured out with intentions of purchasing salted yak-butter tea—a regional drink that Albert had insisted we sample—but after one sip and a lot of hacking, we decided it was best if the tea stayed in the pot. And so we just sat around talking instead.

"Why did you come to Tibet?" Sara asked Amaya.

"Actually, this is sort of a pilgrimage for me too. I want to become a Buddhist nun."

Sara's eyes widened. "Really? That's so *cool!*"

"Explains the haircut," I added. "What inspired you to do that?"

"Well, I've always felt a draw to the spiritual realm. I believe there's so much more to life than what we see. I'm going to go to India next to check out the Buddhist scene there, since that's where I'm from originally."

She went on to tell an incredible story about how she'd been abandoned as an infant on the streets of an Indian metropolis. When rescuers found her, she was riddled with infections and surrounded by dogs, starving, dehydrated, and almost dead.

"It was a miracle that I was saved," she said. "I think about how many kids pass away on the street just like that. Babies who could've grown up to be loving and charismatic, or talented and smart, or even crazy and a jerk—whatever. The point is that so much is just . . ." She snapped her fingers, and we shuddered.

"I was adopted by a secular family in Holland. But I've always been interested in religion. When I learned about the Buddhist philosophy that says to understand the world out there," she spread her hands, "you must first look in here," she pointed to her temple, "it made sense to me. But what about you guys? Are you religious?"

"I wouldn't say I'm religious exactly," said Sara. "But I am spiritual. I definitely believe that there is more to this world than what meets the eye, and that death isn't so much the end as it is a transformation."

Amaya nodded approvingly. "And you?"

I hesitated. Unlike Sara, I didn't have a spiritual side. I'd been raised loosely Catholic but had abandoned the pretenses as a teenager. While I officially cited gay rights, fossil records, and Christopher Hitchens as reason for my renouncement, the truth was that—despite genuine effort—I never sensed the presence that monotheists classify as God. Whenever I prayed, I was overwhelmed by the melancholy and spooky sensation that I was talking to an empty room, and was unable to convince myself of any sort of omnipresent energy unexplainable through science. But now I couldn't help but wonder if I was missing out on something. Did my inability to believe in a higher power mean that I was never going to be at one with the universe—even if only in a psychological sense? Was I depriving myself of bliss and contentment by refusing to accept what, as an atheist, I considered to be harmless untruths?

Amaya stared at me expectantly. Not wanting to get into an uncomfortable debate, I tried to change the subject. "We're going to stay in an ashram when we go to India."

She wasn't fooled by my misdirection, but she smiled anyway. "That'll be interesting. Just remember to do your best to commit to your experience. Be open to whatever is happening around and inside of you."

Religious or not, it was good advice.

- 4 -

Despair, Levitation,
and Television Stardom
in Six Weeks or Less

My grandmother: *Susunka, you cannot go to India. There are too many people there. You won't fit.*

THE HIMALAYAN PEAKS gnashed up at us like sharks' teeth as we soared out of Tibet. Gazing out the window, I entertained smug thoughts about how Sara and I had finally found our traveling groove. It was less than a third of the way into our trip and we'd already teased the delta beasts, scaled the mountain trails, and rubbed elbows with monks (or at least watched them skate across the floor). So what if there had been a few inopportune encounters with sand fleas and wet socks? Those tribulations only made us stronger. Here we were, backpackers extraordinaire, globetrotting at the pace of a happy canter.

Then we landed in India and all my self-assurance went tits-up.

Just leaving the Delhi airport was a mission of gobsmacking proportions. The forty-degree heat was as suffocating as a wet wool blanket. The pollution was so thick that I could practically chew the air. And when we exited from the terminals, the wiggling throng of mustachioed cabbies hollering for our attention and clawing at the loose straps of our bags with spry fingers was nothing short of terrifying. Sara and I stared at them for about six seconds before we spun around and ran back inside.

"There has to be an easier way to do this," she mused.

We looked around and found a pre-paid taxi stand where we were able to purchase a ride for a flat rate. It was more expensive than a meter read would have been, but it saved us the anguish of dealing with the mob. This time when we left the terminal, it was on the heels of a dauntless driver who swept us into his taxi with all limbs, straps, and flip-flops accounted for.

At some point between the Beatles dropping acid in Rajasthan and Lululemon selling inner peace one pair of stretch pants at a time, our hemisphere became infatuated with a romanticized notion of India. Yuppies drink Starbucks chai lattes. Stoners burn Nag Champa incense. Vegans preach antimaterialism to suburbanites trying to put their feet behind their heads. I likewise dreamed of a backpacker holy land where the air smelled like patchouli and tasted like masala, where the ostensible chaos pulsed harmoniously to a national heartbeat, where a palpable elegance permeated the wandering spirit and enveloped the inquiring mind with an enigmatic sense of . . . well, whatever it was that rendered backpackers in awe of the place.

Though after twenty minutes in Delhi, I began wondering if my expectations weren't slightly misguided.

It was dirtier than any city I'd ever seen, dirtier than I thought any city could get. The buildings were caked in generations' worth of dust. Cars and trucks emitted odious farts of brown and blue gas. Mounds of unbagged garbage rotted in the heat, releasing a stench that could gag a maggot. Sure, Kathmandu had been dirty as well. But that dirt was much more manageable—almost cute, actually, in a whimsical, adds-character kind of way. Delhi's dirt, on the other hand, was frightening and aggressive. I could almost see the hepatitis peering at me from the rancid piles of shit.

If there was an underlying national heartbeat, then it suffered from a violent arrhythmia. Taxis and tuk-tuks, rickshaws and rats, beggars and businessmen, and bovines and bicycles with bundles of squawking chickens hanging from the handlebars bustled past our cab. A motorcycle with six people on the seat and a baby held off to the side like a lunch box clipped our side mirror. Traffic was simultaneously bumper to bumper yet dashing off in all directions, and I half hid my eyes behind my fingers as I awaited a splintering, splattering explosion of metal and flesh.

Of course, most jarring were the young children with scarred faces who darted between the cars, rattling tin cups against the dark windows of shining Mercedes-Benzes. On the sidewalks, families plaited hair and prepared meals while the hustling crowd traipsed through their living rooms. Gaunt beggars with twisted bones and stumped limbs wailed from the corners, and although I reminded myself that begging was their livelihood and the theatrics were part of the act, it didn't make it any easier to watch. It wasn't like I hadn't been expecting poverty—I'd read the novels, seen the documentaries, downloaded *Slumdog Millionaire*. But nothing could have adequately prepared me for witnessing it in person.

Two hours later, we clambered out of the cab in Paharganj, Delhi's backpacker district. Exhausted and sweating, we tripped over the crags in the road as we wandered in search of our guest-house. Unfortunately for us, the street was lined with *hundreds* of guesthouses. And when the managers caught sight of our bulging backpacks and sagging spirits, they beckoned, "Right here! This way! Come-come!"

"No thanks, we already have a reservation," said Sara with more civility than I could have mustered when a brazen innkeeper blocked our path.

"I know you do," he scoffed, *paan*-stained spittle flying. "It's over here. Hurry up."

"What are you talking about? You don't know where we're going!" I snapped grouchily. "Don't give me this 'it's over here' bullshit. You're just trying to lure us into your hotel! How dumb do you think we are?"

Sara grabbed my arm and pulled me away. "Come on, Sue. Save your energy."

At long last, we found our guesthouse—wedged in an alleyway between an Internet café and a massage parlor. After dragging our packs up six flights of stairs, we staggered into the room we'd be calling "craphole, sweet craphole" for the night. The walls were covered in goobers and the mattress was bare and stained.

Even the cockroaches refused to scatter when we turned on the light. Instead, they twiddled their antennae mockingly before meandering into the shadows. I took it as an ominous sign.

"Five bucks a night?" Sara ventured weakly.

"Hell is free," I muttered in response.

WE PASSED OUT early that night, which was auspicious because we had to be up again at four thirty AM to catch the train to Agra. As we chugged out of the station beneath a sorbet-colored sky, I thought back to my frustrations of the day before and blushed into my chai. It certainly wasn't the chimerical inauguration I'd imagined while perusing colorful Indian scarves in Toronto's Kensington Market. But perhaps Delhi was an acquired appreciation, like whiskey or sauerkraut. Maybe I needed to work up to it. Surely the delicate splendor of the Taj Mahal would be an easily digestible introduction to India's majesty.

To the smell of patchouli and the taste of masala, I thought, raising my tea in a private toast before taking a sip. "Ow! Fuck!"

"Be careful, it's hot," warned Sara as I scrambled for water to dose my scalded tongue. "Great masala flavor, though."

We disembarked in Agra a couple of hours later and hired a tuk-tuk wallah to drive us to the Taj Mahal. Alas, our visit was unexpectedly delayed when he abruptly skidded to the soft shoulder and refused to continue until we visited his cousin's jewelry emporium. And stone emporium. And carpet emporium.

"This is a lovely weave but I'm just not in the market for a hand-stitched Persian rug," insisted Sara while I batted at the flies. "Can you *please* take us to the Taj Mahal now?"

"The Taj Mahal has been standing for three hundred and fifty years—it is not going anywhere. But with prices so low, this merchandise will vanish like that!" The tuk-tuk wallah snapped his fingers and the store proprietor wobbled his head enthusiastically.

"I'm going to get a Fanta," I announced. "Do you want one?"

Sara nodded, and I wandered over to the snack stand next door. "Two Fantas, please."

The slick-haired teenager grabbed the bottles out of the cooler with one hand and set them on the counter without glancing up from his phone. "Five hundred fifty rupees."

"What? That's like eleven dollars!"

"Okay-okay. Five hundred twenty-five."

By the time we arrived at the world's most celebrated mausoleum, the sun was dipping toward the horizon and the cool marble glowed with a saffron-coral hue. Ornate inlay of semiprecious stones tattooed the walls amid lacy swirls, the florid curlicues eliciting a sense of airy flow and ataractic curvature. Reclining on the lawn with my toes digging into the grass, I released the breath that I'd been unconsciously holding for the past twenty-four hours. "I'm failing at India," I confessed.

Sara leaned back onto one elbow. "What do you mean?"

"Don't get me wrong, this is gorgeous, but—god, I was *so frustrated* today. Between all those emporiums and the ten minutes of haggling over some freakin' pop . . . I know this country is supposed to be backpacker mecca, but it's stressing me out! I just feel like I'm missing something, you know? Like there's this surreptitious beauty that everyone else can see." I sighed. "By the way, you don't need to point out the irony of me staring at the Taj Mahal bitching that I can't find beauty. I'm so ironic, I'm practically Alanis Morissette."

"Technically, it was the situations presented in the song that were ironic, not Alanis herself. And I'm pretty sure some of her music was inspired by India. But anyway, it's only been one day—you have six more weeks to fall in love with the place."

It sounded like a dismayingly long time.

OUR NEXT STOP was Tamil Nadu to visit the ashram. As our tuk-tuk rumbled past roadside snack stands and dusty fields, I wondered if this ashram business was a good idea. What if we were being lured into some sort of cult? What if they brainwashed us into having orgies and signing away all our money? Actually, the orgy bit didn't sound too bad, but I wasn't about to have my trip cut short because a bunch of om-chanting hucksters duped me out of my savings. One thing was certain: if I so much as smelled Kool-Aid, I'd be out of there so fast their auras would spin.

"It's not a cult, it's a spiritual retreat," corrected Sara.

"The only difference between the two is a good public relations rep," I quipped darkly.

"If you think it's a cult, then why are we going?"

"I didn't say it *is* a cult, I said it *might be* a cult. Or it might be just a place where people discover whatever sage wisdom it is that elevates them beyond the petty anxiousness of daily life."

"What's the difference between that and a spiritual retreat?"

Before I could think of an answer, the tuk-tuk suddenly swerved over to the side of the road and ground bumpily to a halt.

"Are we here?" asked Sara.

The driver responded with the head-wobbling gesture I had come to assume meant *yes, no, maybe*, or *I've got water in my ears*.

I leaned forward and peered out the front window with apprehension. We were definitely . . . somewhere. The scraggly fields and snack stands were gone. Our lonesome road was now flanked on both sides by a wooden fence, unbroken save for a lopsided gate. Beyond it, I could see a few low-rise, thatched-roofed buildings and a scattered grove of stumpy trees—but no people. It bore the creepy feeling of an abandoned summer camp.

"Ashram?" I asked. The driver wobbled his head again.

"This must be it," said Sara, climbing out of the tuk-tuk and swinging her backpack onto her shoulders.

"Either that or this is the opening scene of a horror movie."

She ignored me and unlatched the gate. It swung open with a rusty *creeeak*. As we stepped inside, a sudden breeze sent sinister whispers through the dried leaves of the trees. I turned back toward the road but the tuk-tuk driver was already gone, leaving us alone with our thoughts and the snickering leaves . . . and whatever hockey-masked maniacs lurked in the bushes.

"Hello?" called Sara. A dirt path wove between the long dried grass—bleached and matted like the hair of a dead co-ed—and she stepped onto it gingerly. "Is anybody here?"

"I think I've seen this one," I said nervously. "You survive because you're the heroic blonde and I wind up topless and hacked to pieces in the last ten minutes."

She rolled her eyes. "Look, I'm sure this place is fine. It's just low season right now because it's so hot. You've got nothing to worry about."

Just what the heroic blonde would say, I thought—although I noticed her voice trembled.

The breeze returned, sweeping sandy dirt into the air and sending a rattling cackle through the leaves. Branches cracked hollowly, as if someone were rocking on an invisible swing. The sun was bleeding into the horizon, leaving behind shadowy pools that seemed to pulse at the caprice of the wind. My skin prickled with the sensation of eyes. I imagined a legion of brainwashed cult victims clinging to the trees, waiting for us to stumble into their clutches. And then, just when we were too far from the road for anyone to hear our screams they would sneak up behind us and—

"Namaste."

"*Ah!*" I leaped two feet into the air.

"*Ai!*" The young Indian guy jumped back, and the two of us stared at each other with wild eyes and clenched bladders.

"What the *hell!*" he sputtered in a thick, popping accent.

"Don't mind her, she's a little high-strung," Sara glared at me. "Namaste. I'm Sara and this is Sue. We preregistered on your website a few months ago?"

"This way," he replied, shooting me a cautious look before turning his back and leading us into the complex.

The ashram was austere and clean. We dropped our bags in the female dormitory and then hurried upstairs to where the evening activities were already getting started. The room on the second floor (where yoga, meditation, and lectures took place) was spacious with a vaulted, thatched-roof ceiling. The outer walls were waist high, allowing the breeze to drift through. There was a gold-dappled shrine depicting traditional images of blue-skinned Hindu gods alongside portraits of the ashram founders. Tiny candles danced at their feet while saccharine plumes of incense rose up like charmed snakes.

Sara had been right about this being the low season. There was only a handful of other travelers there, and none of them fit the 'shram-jammer image I'd had in mind. There was nary a tie-dyed T-shirt or a Birkenstock sandal in sight, nor did anybody introduce themselves as Prism. In fact, with my dreadlocks, I was the only person who was visibly groovy. Everyone else looked pretty much . . . *normal.*

"Namaste. For those of you who have just joined us, welcome." A short Indian man with gray hair and a round belly sat in the lotus position. "I will be your teacher; you may call me Amit-ji. Now, it is time to begin our nightly chanting and meditation. Please use the pages to follow along."

I gave my cheat sheet a cynical glance. Although it was written out in Roman characters, the chants were actually in Sanskrit. Some of the words were nineteen letters long and seemed as intelligible as a spoonful of Alpha-Getti. But before I had a chance to ask how to pronounce anything, bells, shakers, and other small percussion instruments were handed out, Amit-ji gave a curt nod, and we broke out into a noisy rendition of . . . actually, I have no idea.

"*Om namo bhaga—va? te? -eieieooo!*" I sang, my voice warbling out of key as I struggled not to clap my fingers between my rhythm sticks. "*Om namo bhagavate eieioooo!*"

"It's not *eieio*," hissed Sara under her breath. "Vishnu did not live on Old Macdonald's farm."

I stifled a giggle. "Shh! You're throwing me off!"

"You're saying it wrong!"

"Fine, how would you say it?"

"*Om namo bhagavate aya aya ayyyyaaaa!*" she sang, and while her pitch was better I noticed that she was dinging her bells at all the wrong times.

"That's not it," I whispered. "You're just saying *aya aya aya*. Look at all these other letters in there! There's a *v*, an *s*, a *d*, I think I saw a 5—"

"Those letters are silent."

"What, *all* of them?"

"Girls!" Amit-ji's voice sliced sharply through the chanting. "Please!"

Blushing, we ducked behind our cheat sheets.

"Look, you're doing it wrong *and* you're getting us in trouble," muttered Sara. "This is high school all over again."

"*I'm* getting us in trouble?" Incredulous, I forgot to lower my voice. "It's your bell-ringing that's throwing off the class."

"What's wrong with my bell-ringing?"

"You sound like a wind chime in a hurricane!"

"Girls! *Focus!*" Amit-ji was not impressed.

Sara and I glared at each other before returning to butchering the chants in our respective fashions. Outside, the clouds were gathering. A distant rumble of thunder echoed over the plains like an empty wine bottle rolling across a hardwood floor.

"We will now move on to thirty minutes of meditation," said Amit-ji when the chanting had ceased. "If you have a personal mantra, concentrate on that. If not, you may use the universal mantra, *om*. For those of you who are new, we will talk about meditation during our lesson tomorrow. In the meantime, sit in a comfortable, cross-legged position. Resting your wrists on your knees, form a circle with your thumb and forefinger while relaxing your other fingers outward."

He held up his hand and demonstrated. "This is called the *gyan mudra* and represents the unity of one with the Divine. Good. Draw your focus to the space between your eyebrows, which is where your Third Eye—that which looks into the spiritual realm—resides. Now, take a long, slow breath, and allow your thoughts to pass you by until your mind is clear and peaceful."

I chose not to dwell at that moment on concepts such as the Divine and my Third Eye, and inhaled deeply. The fresh scent of evening reminded me of how happy I was to be out in the countryside. Maybe this ashram thing was a good idea after all. The more I reflected on it, the more I wondered if perhaps India and I had gotten off on the wrong foot. Or if perhaps I just wasn't prepared for the pandemonium that ensues when over a billion people share a home. After all, what else could I have expected from a place where there are thirty languages that each have over a million native speakers, where religious zeal runs as diverse as it does deep, and where the disparity between the haves and the have-nots is so astronomical? No wonder India was doing my head in. Maybe that is why yoga and meditation are intrinsic here—they are necessary tools with which to maintain a sense of calm within the bedlam. If that is the case, then the ashram was not only a good idea, but an essential stop if I was going to appreciate the country like an open-minded, culturally attuned backpacker. Besides, what better place to have an epiphany about what to do with my life than in a space devoted to mystic introspection?

My left butt cheek was starting to go numb. Sneakily, I cracked open one eye to see what everybody else was doing. They all seemed to be deep in meditation, legs crossed and hands mudra'd. Some people appeared perfectly still while others had their mantras dancing silently on their lips.

Oh yeah, the mantra. I needed one of those.

I immediately rejected the option of om. Even though I knew it was considered to be a sacred sound by hundreds of millions of people, I just couldn't help associating it with cheesy television stereotypes. I also nixed *peace* and *relax* because the former was too impersonal and the latter . . . well, there was just something about repeatedly ordering myself to relax that made me want to scream. So what else was there? I contemplated *I think, therefore I am* (too pretentious) and *we are all star stuff* (probably copyrighted), and was trying to remember some of the more provocative fortune cookies I'd eaten (wrong country) when suddenly—and as clearly as if it had been whispered into my Third Ear—I heard the following:

Ebb and flow.

Hmm. That could work. Interpreted tangibly, it could refer to the tides, the seasons, the economy, our breath. Philosophically, it suggested that the only reliable constant in life was the element of change. And there was something soothing about it, something that made me feel in tune with the rhythm of the universe and the cyclical balance necessary for infinite motion.

Damn—an hour in an ashram and already I was thinking like a hippie.

I shifted again (now my leg was numb all the way down to my toes and my lower back was beginning to cramp) and took another breath. All right, I was officially pro-ashram, I had my mantra ready to go—time to get down to business. Commencing mental clarity and emotional bliss in T minus three . . . two . . .

Ebb and flow. Ebb and flow. Ebb—

". . . And open your eyes," Amit-ji's voice wafted through the air like curling incense smoke. "Welcome back."

Crap. So much for today's meditation. Oh well, I still had thirteen days to go. I'd definitely get the hang of it by then. After all, wasn't meditation just not thinking? Teachers and parents had been accusing me of that ever since I ate that tube of Lip Smacker when I was a kid—I was probably *way* ahead of the curve. Poor Sara, actually using her brain like an idiot all these years. And what had it gotten her? Well, a lucrative career and a stable future. But we'd just see who reached enlightenment first.

And her bell-ringing really did suck.

OUR DAILY SCHEDULE for the next two weeks included *sat-sang*, which is chanting and meditation, and *asana*, which is the physical exercise that most Westerners think of when they hear the word "yoga." In addition to regular chai breaks, we ate ayurvedic food with our hands while sitting crossed-legged on the floor in what was meant to be total silence.

"Do you think the reason why we don't have any spoons is because all the gurus bent them with their minds?" I whispered to Sara over lunch.

"*Shh!*" scolded Amit-ji.

Our first asana class turned out to be harder than I'd expected. As Toronto boasts about as many yoga studios as it does fire hydrants, I had inevitably attended a multitude of classes over the years. And while I was no Gumby, my dogs had been acceptably downward facing, and my cobras neither hissed nor spat. However, something perturbing had occurred in the months since I'd left home. Sara insisted that my muscles were just tight from the trek, but I was convinced that my legs had gotten longer while my arms—mysteriously and without permission—had shrunk. Whatever the case, my toes were now miles away from my fingertips, and any stretching filled me with the fear of a sudden and unforgiving *snap*.

"What are you doing? Bend!" commanded Amit-ji as we sat on the floor with our legs straight out in front of us, reaching for our feet.

"I am bending!" I squeaked.

"Are you? Never have I seen such a young person so inflexible." He clicked his tongue. "Look at Will, he is twice your age and yet he folds so nicely."

The fifty-plus-year-old lifted his head from his knees and beamed at us from across the room.

"Come on, Sue, it isn't hard," said Sara. She reached her arms above her head and then gently leaned forward until her stomach was only a butterfly's kiss from the top of her thighs. "You just need to relax."

Pfft. There was an invisible sadist holding a blowtorch to the backs of my knees and she was telling me to *relax*? I strained harder, but my hamstrings would not relent.

"Okay class, time for headstands. With your forearms on the floor and your hands clasped in a fist behind your head, use your abdominal muscles to raise your legs—Susan, what sort of asana are you doing? This is supposed to be a still pose!"

"I know!" I cried as my legs flapped like laundry in the wind. "I'm just trying to get my—*waa!*"

But at least this time I wasn't the only person who couldn't manage the position. Sara's attempt devolved into a series of unintentional somersaults, and even Will couldn't get it up. Er—wait, that didn't come out right.

But despite the challenges of asana, what really worried me was our first lecture. I had *no* idea what to expect. Was this Amit-ji's license to get preachy and attempt to win some converts? Or was this the moment he busted out the Quaaludes and assigned us our new identities?

Sara pulled a notebook I'd never seen before out of her backpack.

"What's that for?" I asked.

"Duh, for taking notes!" she replied. "This *is* supposed to be a learning experience, you know. Which do you think is more Zen: the blue pen or the purple pen?"

I rolled my eyes. Freakin' keener.

As it turned out, my reservations were unwarranted. Amit-ji's first topic was simply a translation and discussion of the term "yoga." He explained how, while the West had come to associate the word strictly with the physical practice (asana), its literal meaning was "union." This referred to the process of becoming enlightened by uniting with the Divine.

My eyebrows sprouted skyward like spring crocuses.

"For those of you who don't like the word 'Divine,' think of it as simply uniting with the universe," said Amit-ji, and my brows retreated sheepishly back into their chrysalides. "Remember, we—everything that you see, everything that exists—are all fundamentally made of the same material. Whether you choose to interpret that material as a spiritual energy or in terms of protons and electrons, it amounts to the same idea.

"Right now, you see the world in terms of duality," he continued. "There is you, and there is everything else. That part of you that chooses to see yourself as separate is fueled by your ego. The key to enlightenment is in understanding that if you break it down far enough, you are of the same energy as everything else. Therefore, you are actually part of everything else. There is no separation—you are one with the universe, one with God. And that is the union that yoga is referring to."

I blinked. This was actually making sense. And I was even more impressed with the practical approach he took to meditation:

"A person's mind is like a monkey: always chattering and fidgeting," he said. "We have many unnecessary thoughts running through our heads. Sometimes they are negative, but most of the time they are just pointless and distracting. Meditation teaches us to be aware of these thoughts and overcome them. Its purpose is to calm down that monkey so we can think clearer and become more focused. If you can master staying in the present while sitting quietly, then it will be easier for you to remain calm and in control of yourself during stressful or overwhelming situations."

Well, *that* certainly was logical. I thought of how often my inner monologue rambled on about something silly or useless, blaring like a television in an empty room. Or how I'd get so worked up over something inevitable that the preceding anxiety would end up more stressful than the event itself. Our tour in Africa was the perfect example: I was forever freaking out about how everything was trying to eat me—and yet here I was, perfectly unscathed! Although Kendra and I *did* get stalked by lions, but . . . whatever, there was a point in there somewhere.

I tried to keep Amit-ji's discourse in mind that evening during satsang. Taking a deep breath, I crossed my legs and rested my hands in gyan mudra on my knees. Closing my eyes, I concentrated my energy on my new mantra and ordered the monkey in my head to sit down and shut up.

Ebb and flow. Ebb and flow. Ebb and flow . . .

Incredibly, it started to work. Muscles I didn't know I had engaged—my jaws clenched together, my tongue pressed against the roof of my mouth—softened and released. My breathing slowed. A warm sense of tranquility began to creep at the edges of my mind as if my brain was sinking into a hot bath. Up until now, I'd written meditation off as dippy hocus-pocus or just a successful rebranding of the nap. But now I wondered if there wasn't something to it, after all. If I start meditating on a regular basis, how long would it take before I noticed a difference in day-to-day life? Would Sara and I leave the ashram with some sort of transcendental glow? And if we kept up the habit for the rest of the year, would we return to Toronto blissful and focused? Although, if I was going to keep meditating at home, I'd have to pick up some candles and incense. How did they make incense, anyway? Wasn't it just dried flowers and spices pressed onto a stick? I'd have to look it up. Hey, maybe I could find the instructions to make my own! Then I could just buy some flowers and come up with different incense recipes . . . I could even sell them online! The scents would be inspired by the ashram and all my badass meditation skills—

". . . And open your eyes."

Goddammit!

"Mmm, that felt amazing," said Sara as we headed back to the dorms. Her voice was like whipped butter. "I'm really starting to get the hang of it. How did you do?"

I sighed. "I spent so much time thinking about meditating that I forgot to actually meditate."

"You have to learn to let go of your thoughts. Just *chill.*"

"First you're telling me to harden the fuck up, now you're telling me to chill. Which is it?" I snapped, a little more testily than I'd intended to.

But she just laughed and shook her head. "Oh, Sue." Then she glided off toward the showers, leaving me to wonder what I was screwing up this time.

SARA'S JOURNAL: ASHRAM, day three: *Feeling very tranquil. Concentrating on observing and being present. Was able to sit* through entire meditation without moving today, time flew by. Asana is still challenging but flexibility is improving as I become more aware of my body. Today's mindful intention: "Let go."

My journal: Ashram, day three: *Christ, are we done yet? "Let go, let go." Let go of fucking what? And how can you really let go of something, anyway? As long as you have your memories, you have the opinions and emotions that are attached to them. It's not like you can suddenly throw out a thought or an experience the way you would an old shoe. Utter nonsense. Also, my body hurts from yoga—sorry, "asana"—and I still can't do a stupid headstand.*

Sara's journal: *Ashram, day four. Thoughts are becoming increasingly clear and more direct. Have stopped worrying about what Mom thinks of my trip. She is who she is and I cannot change her. Must practice empathy and remember to hold space for her emotions. Today's mindful intention: "Be present."*

My journal: *Ashram, day five (morning). I take it all back— this place is great! I woke up this morning feeling, oh-em-gee, like I was on ecstasy!! Still can't focus during* ebb-and-flow-ebb-and-flow-ebb-and-flow *(say it fast, sounds like "elbow") but who cares? Life is amazing!*

My journal: *Ashram, day five (evening). So hollow, so empty. I ache as the vacuum within threatens to collapse my body's empty shell. We all live inside our heads. We have no clue what everyone else experiences. The notion of union with another is false; the idea that we can even begin to understand who someone else is—on a level so fundamental that it is indescribable—is a delusion. Our consciousness is just a pod, an aquarium from which we peer out at a world we can never truly touch. WE ARE ALL UTTERLY ALONE. We may all be made of the same components on an atomic level, but the vast majority of an atom is empty space.*

". . . And open your eyes."

We had closed our eyes to a world cloaked in the inky shadows of night. But when we opened them again thirty minutes later, champagne sunshine spilled into the room in bubbling golds and fizzing pinks. Even in my melancholy state, I could appreciate the elegance of the morning.

The others gathered themselves, sleepy and introspective, and made their way downstairs to where the chai was waiting. But I held back. Amit-ji was arranging marigold heads on the altar and I approached him with my eyes cast down.

"Sorry, may I talk to you about something?" My voice wavered with defeat.

"Of course." He turned around. "What is on your mind?"

"Well, I'm not sure how to say this, but . . . Okay, I know all this meditation is supposed bring us peace. But the truth is that it's having the opposite effect on me. I've been getting these *crazy* mood swings. Irritability over nothing, giddiness to the point of mania, depression that feels like it's swallowing me from within." I took an embarrassed breath. "Is there something wrong with me? Am I, like, royally messing this up? Do you think it would be better if I just left?"

I had expected Amit-ji to be disappointed or perhaps even cross with me. But instead he chuckled, wagging his head back and forth like a dashboard figurine. "Oh, Susan. It is natural to have these feelings, isn't it?"

"Isn't it?" I was confused. "I mean, is it?"

"Of course it is! Think: if you were given the task to clean up and reorganize a cluttered room, what would be the first thing you would do?"

"Er . . ." Was this a trick question? "I guess take everything out of it?"

"Exactly!" He slapped his belly for emphasis. "And that is just what you have to do with a cluttered mind. Sometimes, when a person begins to meditate, he will experience painful or confusing emotions that seem to come out of nowhere. That is just your mind purging itself. It is a good thing, isn't it? It will pass."

I sighed. I certainly hoped so, because my emotions hadn't yo-yoed this much since puberty. I couldn't decide if it felt like I was on drugs, or coming off of drugs, or in need of drugs, or *what*. I thanked Amit-ji and then headed downstairs.

"How's it going, Sue?" asked Will. He was a cheerful Malaysian man with large glasses and a shaved head. The two of us had taken to chatting during teatime.

"Ugh. I'm having some issues." I poured myself a cup of chai. "Can I be honest with you about something?"

"Of course."

"I don't believe in a higher consciousness. Or a soul. Or an afterlife. Or that life has any sort of meaning beyond that which we choose to give it." I exhaled. "You think I'm crazy for coming to an ashram, don't you?"

"I think it was an unusual decision for an atheist," he agreed. "What did you hope to get out of your time here?"

"I don't know. I mean, people journey to India to become enlightened—enlightened in regard to *what*, exactly, I still have no clue. Anyway, I guess I was wondering if that experience is possible for someone who doesn't accept all the other spiritual stuff that typically goes along with it."

"Is it?"

"If it is, then I'm definitely nowhere close." I dabbed my finger-tip into the skin that had formed on my chai, and it grabbed hold like a tiny creature.

Will fell quiet for a moment. "You agree that some people reach this state, yes?" he asked at last.

"Yeah, I think so."

"But if you don't believe there's a mystical component to it, then you must attribute the notion of enlightenment to a grand mental shift—to gaining significant control over your own thoughts and emotions."

"Yes."

"Do you think anybody has accomplished that in a week?"

I hesitated, but before I could respond the bell signaled it was time for asana.

I guzzled down the rest of my tea and hurried upstairs. As we ran through our series of sun salutations, I contemplated what Amit-ji and Will had said. There was certainly *something* taking place inside my brain—maybe Amit-ji was right in that it was just a sort of spring-cleaning. And Will definitely had a point when he implied that I was expecting too much in such a short time period. Even though Sara was evidently achieving some sort of internal harmony, it wasn't a competition. Perhaps I needed to just continue focusing on the task without becoming too hung up on the results.

"Susan! Excellent headstand! Well done!" Amit-ji clapped.

"Nice!" exclaimed Sara when I had righted myself. "How'd you do that?"

"I don't know. I just sort of followed the steps—solid arm placement, lifting with my abs—and didn't really think about where it was going to lead me." I blinked as the blood rushed out of my head. "Hey, can you take a picture of me doing it next time?"

"I'm pretty sure that goes against the whole let-go-of-your-ego thing."

"What? Oh, that's so *lame!*"

Will and Amit-ji exchanged a look. "Baby steps," sighed the Malaysian.

I'D LIKE TO say that Will's offhand counsel was exactly what I needed to achieve enlightenment after all. Regrettably, that was not to be. By the end of our stay, the ashram felt less like a torturous mental experiment and more like day camp at an alternative school. Although I retained all the flexibility of a crowbar, I turned out to be surprisingly decent at head-, hand-, and elbow-stands. And while I never actually slipped into a meditative trance, my feet didn't go quite as numb anymore. However, the lectures did inevitably take a strange turn, and I concluded (not without the bitter satisfaction of a cynic proven correct) that my previous suspicions about the place weren't *totally* unwarranted.

"Now, class, you may have heard people discuss tricks such as levitation or bending spoons with your mind. Let me assure you that the gurus are very much capable of all this and more," said Amit-ji. "But it wouldn't be humble for them to show off like circus people. So they keep it to themselves."

I glanced over at Sara. She didn't meet my eye but she did stop writing, her pen poised above the page.

"Extreme physical cleanliness is also very important to yogis," Amit-ji continued. "You might shower every day, sometimes even twice, but there are parts of your body you are missing. Like your nasal cavity. Watch and learn." As we looked on in bemusement, Amit-ji fed a piece of cotton string in one nostril and out the other, then pulled it back and forth until it was covered in goobers.

I elbowed Sara in the ribs. "No wonder I couldn't attain inner peace. I hadn't flossed my nose yet."

She sighed and closed her notebook.

Although the ashram was ultimately a positive experience for the most part, I was nevertheless stoked when the time came to move onward. After two weeks of wrestling with the demons that tormented my mind and constricted my hamstrings, I felt psychologically equipped and emotionally eager to face the "real" India again. But first, we were headed for a backpacker oasis in Kerala, a southern state known for its lush landscapes and laissez-faire attitude. As we made our way across the countryside, the surroundings transformed from dusty brush to fields of palms. Vegetation sprouted and swelled around lazy rivers and the forest was suddenly bursting at the seams, spilling onto the road in a tangled mess.

Our destination was Varkala Beach, which featured a gigantic rock-faced cliff overlooking the ocean where the sunlight flickered upon the waves like millions of drowning fireflies. Hugging the edge were hippie-style coffee shops with patrons lounging on floor pillows and gentle electronica crackling through the speakers. Below was a massive beach where Western twentysomethings swam and sunbathed in bikinis.

"It's not very authentically Indian," Sara observed with disappointment.

"Maybe they make curry-flavored martinis," I said, my enthusiasm for the "real" India momentarily surpassed by my excitement for pizza.

Two hours, four *lassis* (a yogurt-based drink), and one over-priced-but-totally-worth-it pizza later, we were strewn across the sand with cirrus clouds reflecting in our sunglasses.

"Now this is my idea of inner peace," I said as I stretched my arms above my head.

Sara dog-eared her page in *Shantaram*. "Yeah. It may not be culturally inspiring, but it sure is nice. Hey, look! I think they're filming something over there."

I rolled over and propped myself up on my elbows. Sure enough, there was a camera crew gathered around a volleyball net where four oiled-up male models were frolicking about in the tightiest of whities.

"I can see their abs from here!" Sara exclaimed.

"It's not their abs I'm looking at."

"What? *Oh!* Oh, those have got to be tube socks or something."

"If that's what the average Indian man is packing, I'm beginning to understand why they've got a population problem."

We giggled and returned to our repose. When our stomachs began to rumble again, we gathered our belongings and climbed back up the rocky staircase to the top of the cliff in search of dinner. Soon we found a place with paper lanterns hanging from the rafters and candles propped up in empty wine bottles, and sat down on the patio.

I scanned the menu. "I think I'm going to order pizza again."

"Oh my god, Sue!"

"Hey, it's my vacation too, you know."

"No—*look!* It's the models from the beach!"

I dropped the menu and spun around in my seat. Sure enough, the male models we'd spied on earlier were gathered at a table near the back of the restaurant. They were talking with a small group of backpackers—two girls in sundresses and three guys with dark tans and bright smiles.

"We've *got* to go sit with them!" I jumped up.

"Wait a second!" Sara grabbed my arm. "You can't just walk over there. What are you going to say?"

"Come on, I'm sure they're not going to complain that a couple of chicks in bikinis want to chat. Besides, when else are you going to get the chance to rub elbows with Mumbai's finest?"

"I doubt they're Mumbai's *finest*."

"Even better—then there's no reason at all to be intimidated. Let's go!" Before she could reply, I marched over and inserted myself at the end of the table.

". . . But of course the photographer's memory card is full, and we all know where the spare was!" one of the models was saying. I chimed in with the polite laughter that ensued.

"Hope you don't mind if we join you," I whispered to the girl

I'd sat down next to. "My friend and I were watching them film on the beach earlier. When we saw that they were in here, *obviously* we had to come say hello."

"Hah, that's exactly what my sister and I did," she whispered back. "It's an underwear commercial, by the way. These lads are in it too." She gestured to the three white guys across from us.

"Really? Are they models as well?"

"No, they're just French." She explained how they had been recruited as extras by the director. "It's pretty common to use travelers in commercials because they're willing to work for free."

"Apparently they didn't get much done today, though," her sister chimed in. "Most of it will happen tomorrow. So we'll have plenty of entertainment while we work on our tans."

"I see we have some newcomers," one of the models grinned at us. Sara blushed.

"Hope we're not interrupting anything. We saw you guys shooting and it was pretty cool to watch," I said. "So we thought we'd come over and say hi."

"Hey, welcome! The more the merrier."

And that was how we ended up having dinner with Indian underwear models. They were very friendly, although one man— the elder of the group at forty years old and with a physique that implied he was more of an actor than a model—kept fluttering his eyelashes at me in a way that may have been seductive by Bollywood standards but seemed a bit over the top to me.

"My name's Billy. And I'm kind of a big deal in Mumbai."

I snorted into my lassi.

The models were fun, but we spent most of the dinner talking to the two sisters, Hannah and Rebecca. They were from London and the same age as us. They introduced us to the other Englander, a guy named Kevin, and the two (cough) extremely attractive (cough) Frenchmen, Jacques-René and Sebastian.

"*Viens-tu du Canada? Tu parles français?*" Jacques-René asked.

"Huh?" I blinked. "Sorry, one more time?"

"*Laisse tomber.*"

The models headed home after dinner ("You don't get a face like this from doing tequila shots all night," Billy said to me with a wink), but we decided to stay and have a drink with the others. Sure enough, one drink led to two, two drinks led to nine, and the next thing I knew I was a giggling, dribbling mess.

"You can say anything in French and it sounds sexy," I slurred as I gestured to the waiter for another vodka/soda. "Like, you could read out a recipe for tuna casserole and I'll be all *yeah baby.*"

"*L'anglais n'est pas une langue très romantique. À vous entendre parler en croirait les Simpsons,*" replied Jacques-René. "*Hum . . . je voulais dire, j'aime bien tes cheveux.*"

"That's *so hot,*" I whispered to Hannah. She grinned and nodded in agreement, discreetly sliding her hand up Sebastian's thigh.

WE AWOKE THE next morning with splitting heads and roiling stomachs.

"It could be worse," said Sara as she opened the drapes, sending me scrambling for my sunglasses. "At least we're not soaking wet in a truck this time."

We had agreed to meet Hannah, Rebecca, and Kevin for breakfast. As it turned out, they were in equally rough shape, and conversation was stilted until we finished our Bloody Caesars. But the hair of the dog did its job—we soon felt well enough to venture down to the beach and see how the commercial was coming along.

"Sue! Good morning!" Billy waved. "You've come to see the magic happen!"

I watched as a makeup artist drew on his abdominal lines with bronzer. "Uh . . . yeah, something like that."

"Excellent. You *have* to meet our director, by the way. He's an absolute *vis*-ionary. Ajay!" He cupped his hands and called across the set. "Hey, Ajay! Come meet my friends!"

The director—a bald man with a cigarette that hung over his lower lip much in the same manner that his paunch hung over his Bermuda shorts—bumbled over. We politely said hello, and he gave us the elevator stare. "You girls ever been in a commercial before?"

"*What!*" Rebecca gasped as the rest of us squealed under our breaths. "You mean . . . you want us to . . . ?"

"We need some more extras. Go stand over there by the volleyball court and when we yell *action*, starting cheering." He glanced at Sara's cleavage. "And make sure you jump up and down a lot."

The plot of the commercial was that the three models were challenged to a volleyball game by Billy, Jacques-René, and Sebastian. As we cheered them on, the models—who were all wearing the brand-name underwear—humiliated their rivals in a flamboyant and almost slapstick victory. It was the corniest thing I'd ever seen and I was thrilled to be a part of it.

"*Action!*" yelled Ajay.

We whooped and screamed and bounced up and down, although Sara kept her arms firmly pinned in front of her chest.

"Aaaaaaand *cut*! Where's Makeup? Their stomachs are melting off!"

"So what else is a product of, ah, Bollywood magic?" I asked one of the models.

He looked down at his groin. "What, this? Don't worry, baby, this is all me."

Billy must've overheard us because, all of a sudden, he whipped the volleyball at the model's crotch. It bounced off his underwear and rolled into the ocean before the model could fake a flinch. Sara and I stifled a laugh.

They filmed until the sun disappeared behind the cliff and the shadows grew long. By then, our shoulders were burned and our voices were hoarse, but we were still giddy as hell. A men's underwear commercial, of all things! In India! Screw shark diving, now *this* was a Facebook status.

The crew was having a celebratory dinner that evening and Ajay invited us to come along. The second we arrived, however, Billy grabbed me by the elbow and dragged me over to sit beside him. He then started laying on so much cheese that I nearly developed lactose intolerance. The only person who could get a word in edgewise was the waiter asking if I'd like another drink (the answer to which was always a desperate *yes*).

Around eleven o'clock, there was an abrupt crack of thunder that caused the glasses to rattle and the diners to jump. An electrical storm had begun across the ocean. We abandoned our plates and scurried to the cliff's edge to watch the spectacle before the rains began. Pink forks shot sideways across the sky like veins running through the clouds. Purple bolts sprouted up from the water like winter trees. As my head reeled from the flashes, I realized that I was much tipsier than I'd intended to be. Trying to stay cool, I nonchalantly leaned against a low stone wall to keep myself from *waa*'ing right over the edge.

"This is stunning!" exclaimed Hannah as everything went blindingly white, then dizzyingly black. Kaleidoscopic spots danced in front of our eyes.

"God gives us beautiful things," said Billy. "Beautiful storms for beautiful souls. Beautiful men for beautiful women . . ." He leaned against the stone wall next to me.

· I hiccupped.

"Gosh, we are so fortunate," said Sara as Kevin draped his arm across her shoulders. "We spent all afternoon pretending to be movie stars in an actual commercial, and now nature is providing us with this amazing storm. It's been such a memorable day."

Billy whispered in my ear, "Want to make it a memorable night?"

"I have to pee!" I announced loudly.

Making my best effort not to wobble, I ducked away from the group and raced back to the restaurant. I had to get myself together, and *quick*. I did *not* want to go home with Billy. Even though it *had* been three months on the road now and I hadn't met *anybody* to . . . I mean, that's a *long time* and . . . but no. He wasn't even that attractive, for Christ's sake! Sure, he was famous (ish) and it would make for a good story but—*no*. This was not the time for my loins to get the better of me.

"*Oh! Excusez-moi!*" Lost in thought, I crashed into Jacques-René outside the bathrooms. "*Susanne, tu vas trébucher! Combien de verres as-tu bus?*"

He grabbed me around the waist to keep me from falling. God, he was strong! *He* certainly didn't need any bronzer on his abs. My breath caught in my throat.

A coy smile tugged at the corner of his lips. "*Laver et arranger le poisson,*" he said in a low, sultry voice. "*Dans une poêle, faire chauffer le beurre et l'huile . . .*"

At that moment, lightning split the sky directly above our heads and the rain poured out. The water droplets gathered on our eyelashes and cascaded down our cheeks like tears. Jacques-René still had his hands on my waist.

"Come to my room?" he whispered.

"Sue!" I could hear Billy calling me from the cliffside as he and the others scrambled for shelter. "Where are you?"

"Let's go! Quick!" I cried. He grinned and grabbed my hand, and the two of us ran to his guesthouse. Inside his room, he handed me a towel and then lit the tea lights that had been arranged on a bookshelf.

Leave it to a Frenchman to backpack with tea lights, I thought.

The next thing I knew, we were kissing fiercely as Massive Attack murmured through his iPod speakers. He lifted me up and threw me backward onto the bed with a devilish smile. I raised my hips so he could slide off my shorts, and he was on me in an instant, his hands, his lips, his—

"*Ooh la la!*" he cried as I wrapped my legs around him. "*Ooh la la!*"

"Well I guess *you* weren't wearing a tube sock," was my drunken response.

IT WASN'T LONG before we were on the road again—gazing out the windows of trains, buses, and tuk-tuks as our thoughts danced like spiders on a pond. Through Alleppey, where the women laundered and bathed in the backwaters; through Kochi, where the Chinese fishing nets towered like praying mantises over the sea; through Munnar, where the mist caught in the treetops like cobwebs. We boarded a sleeper train and rode twenty hours on fold-down bunks, waking to find seventeen children staring at us in bewilderment.

Our final destination was one of the country's most iconic cities, arguably the India-est place in India: Kolkata. It was also the perfect opportunity to redeem myself after my precarious start in Delhi—I could finally earn my India backpacker badge by going with the flow and staying grounded in the teeming metropolis. (While the sentiment was intended metaphorically, I had seen some embroidered patches for sale in the markets that would look awesome stitched onto my day bag.)

At first, I did okay. When I saw the stray dogs lapping at the blood that trickled out of the Muslim butcher shops where cow heads gaped with wall-eyes and lolling tongues, I continued to the aromatic *dosa* stalls where we dined on fermented crepes and coconut chutney. When I whiffed the noxious stench of the toxic gray sludge that oozed through the open sewers, I directed my attention to the dazzling mosaic of glitter and glass that was the bangle vendor's wares. But when we were accosted by swollen-bellied street children who yanked on our Ali Baba pants and mimed that they were hungry, I was at a complete loss for what to do. And when I caught a glimpse of a horrifically burned beggar women, I felt the wind *whoosh* from my lungs.

Her nose had been reduced to a weeping gash and her lips did not extend beyond her gums, baring her teeth in a permanent, unwilling grin. In lieu of hair and ears were knots of scar tissue. All traces of her left eye were gone—unbroken skin stretched taut over the socket—while her right was runny and wholly undistinguishable. Yet the hands that clenched her bowl of alms revealed the suppleness of youth, and I realized she couldn't have been any older than I was.

All of the fear and stress I had kept dammed since Delhi rushed back like a tidal wave, sweeping away whatever meager headway I'd made at the ashram. I thought back to what Amit-ji had said about remaining present in the moment and was struck by the staggeringly obvious question I hadn't thought to ask: what if that moment was shitty and terrifying and agonizing?

The beggar woman rattled her bowl and suddenly my stomach cramped as though caught in a bear trap, and I raced back to our guesthouse as quickly as my clenched butt cheeks would allow.

- 5 -

Piratical Magic

Kyle: *I always wanted to become a pirate when I grew up. So I did.*

F GOING FROM Zimbabwe to Kathmandu was like doing a line of cocaine and being hit with a frying pan, then going from Kolkata to Hanoi was like taking a shot of gasoline and getting a pony for Christmas. As we made our way from Arrivals to Baggage, Sara and I squealed over the small luxuries we had once taken for granted.

"Check out the bathrooms! There's actually *soap*!"

"This floor is so clean I can look up my own shorts!"

"Holy crap, is that a *garbage can*? I haven't seen one of those in months! Let's hug it."

During our flight, we had sat next to Mike—a Canadian in his mid-twenties who had recently moved to the Philippines. He laughed at our unbridled enthusiasm toward Southeast Asia ("Oh my god! The airplane meal is *noodles*!"), although he was appalled that his new homeland wasn't on our itinerary. Determined to change our minds, he raved about the powdery beaches, flourishing sea life, and friendly locals.

"I'm telling you, it's the best-kept secret of backpacking," he insisted. "*Everybody* does the mainland circuit, and then hits Bali for a week or two. In a few years, the Philippines are going to be on that route too—it's too beautiful *not* to be—so you had better go now before it's completely ruined by commercialization." He added that while Boracay wasn't exactly a hidden paradise anymore, regions like Palawan remained unspoiled by excessive tourism.

"We'll pencil it in," said Sara as Noi Bai International Airport popped into view and the landing gear clunked into place.

Vietnam turned out to be a whirlwind of quintessential Asia—or at least what I imagined quintessential Asia to be. We began in the old quarter of the city where the buildings were adorned with antiquated teak balconies and the streets hummed with motorcycle traffic. Scramblers taxied us to our guesthouse—Sara balancing with casual grace and me clinging to my driver in fear of toppling off the back with my bag and landing in the road like an upturned beetle. On the sidewalks, locals gathered around food stalls on child-sized plastic furniture to dine on pho and steamed snails. Old ladies in conical hats carried bamboo poles across their shoulders with produce-filled baskets hanging from each end. The city felt safe and clean, and we explored with a carefree confidence that we hadn't felt back in India.

From Hanoi we journeyed to the mountain town of Sa Pa, where fog meandered down the alleyways like a lost tourist, and the valley walls were ribbed with rice paddies. The moment we got off the train, we were besieged by teenaged girls from the neighboring Black H'Mong and Red Dzao hill tribes. Dressed in black hats and embroidered skirts, they hawked postcards and bracelets with brassy ferocity. We soon discovered that not a single Westerner went anywhere in town without a handful of these giggling escorts, all crooning, "You buy from *meeeee*! You buy from nobody but *meeeee*! You *promiiiiiise*!"

The backstreets of Sa Pa teemed with exotic grocery markets. Live toads and snakes wiggled and slithered in basins of water. Gigantic jars housed pickled pythons while smaller ones contained scorpions and worms. Squirrels could be purchased dried and flattened as if they had been scraped off an Arizona highway. But what really caught my eye were the severed heads and paws of dogs.

"You are creepy and weird," observed Sara as I snapped photo after photo.

"I'm a vegetarian, I'm allowed to be creepy and weird. You're the one who's probably eating the stuff. How sure are you that that's *really* beef in your pho?"

She rolled her eyes, although when it came time for lunch she ordered a salad.

Next, we journeyed to Ha Long Bay, where limestone isles towered above the lapping waves and shadowed caves bared their stalactites like fangs. Residents of Ha Long Bay's traditional floating villages fished off the side of their brightly colored houseboats— although now their livelihood relied just as heavily on tourism as it did on the sea's bounty. Sara and I traveled around the bay aboard a pirate-themed "party boat" operated by a major hostel in Hanoi. Therefore, in addition to kayaking below the karsts and slipping on guano in the grottos, we also drank ourselves delirious alongside fifteen other giggling, sunburned backpackers.

Finally, we rambled south along the coast to Củ Chi , which lay just beyond Ho Chi Minh City. Surrounded by balmy jungle and chattering tour groups, we posed for photos on top of a rusting army tank and wandered through an exhibit of Viet Cong booby traps. Below our feet were the Củ Chi tunnels, part of the massive tunnel network that ran beneath much of Vietnam. In addition to providing communication and supply routes for Viet Cong soldiers during the war, they had functioned as the food and weapons cache—as well as being a home and a hospital.

"You're kidding me," I huffed as we crawled on our hands and knees through the portion of the tunnels that was open to the public. The air was thick with shadow and dampness, and I felt like I'd just been swallowed by a gigantic stone python. "I have difficulty turning around in here, and you're telling me that people actually *lived* in these tunnels?"

"And just think: this section has been widened for our fat Western butts!" replied Sara. "Imagine how tiny it must've been back then."

I did—and regretted it immediately. "Christ. Okay, while the sensation of being buried alive is apparently your idea of a swell afternoon, it isn't mine. I'm going to crawl out that emergency exit hatch over there. I'll see you on the other side."

As we rode the bus into Ho Chi Minh City, Sara mentioned that we needed to decide where we were flying to next, and I agreed. We had seen all we'd intended to see in Vietnam—another country, another passport stamp. Yet I was suddenly overcome with a vague sense of dissatisfaction. While running around what had once been a battleground had been pretty fucked up, it'd failed to leave more than a fleeting impression on me. I had the strange sensation of being in a postcard—everything was beautiful, yet somehow flat.

Sara felt the same way. "So Vietnam was fun . . ."

"But . . . ?"

"I don't know. In India we were in the underwear commercial, and in Nepal we threw up with our dads. But here we just checked off the sights in the guidebook. I mean, it was nice and all—and I'm certainly grateful we didn't puke—but I have to confess, it doesn't feel like we did anything that unique."

I nodded; I'd been thinking the exact same thing. It seemed like *everybody* we met in Vietnam was following an identical route along the sea. Our stories matched their stories. And while it was fun to share a laugh at a dried squirrel now and again, the commonality of it was a little disappointing. After all, had we *really* traveled all this way just to become one of the herd?

Sara sighed. "I suppose it's naive of us to think that our trip would be completely special. So many Southeast Asian countries thrive on tourism—clearly we're not the only ones here."

"But that doesn't mean we can't get off the beaten path," I countered. "So what if it's super touristy? We've just got to be diligent about not coasting along with everyone else, that's all. Make sure this stays an adventure instead of becoming a vacation."

She considered this. "Well, in that case, maybe we should take Mike's advice and visit the Philippines next."

"I was just thinking that! And when we get to Boracay, we'll try *extra* hard to find weird shit to do."

As it turned out, we didn't have to try very hard after all.

OUR PLANS FOR Southeast Asia were hardly set in stone and travel between the countries was easy, so it was no problem for us to add a three-week detour. It *was* a problem for Sara's mother, however.

Within twenty-four hours of our decision, Sara's inbox exploded with emails shrieking at us in all caps. Apparently, some religious turbulence in Mindanao had provoked the Canadian embassy to issue a travel advisory for the entire country. Despite the fact that we weren't going anywhere near Mindanao, Jean was convinced we were on a suicide mission and lashed out at her daughter accordingly.

This trip has changed you. I don't even know who you are anymore, she wrote in one particularly scathing message.

"For fuck's sake, Mom! I'm twenty-four-years-old! I can take care of myself!" Sara yelled back at the computer screen. A couple of people in the Internet café turned to stare, but she was too upset to notice.

"I guess we now know what constitutes a 'questionable' country," I offered.

"My entire life, I've been *so responsible*." Sara continued, ignoring my attempt at levity. "I never did hard drugs or pierced my face. I never rebelled. I never talked back. I worked like hell in university to make my parents proud. And for what? It obviously hasn't proven *anything* to her, because here she is freaking out as if I were just some stupid child."

Her eyes glistened wetly and I quickly said, "We don't *have* to go to the Philippines. It's not a big deal."

"But I *want* to go!" Her voice cracked. "The point is that I'm a capable adult *and* I'm paying for this trip myself. Therefore, she has *no right* to tell me where I can and cannot go . . ."

"But . . . ?"

"But she's my mother, and I love her. God, she's taking this so *personally.*" Tears spilled onto her cheeks, and she wiped at them angrily. "This is worse than when I told her about the trip in the first place. I should've known it wouldn't end there."

I had no idea what to say. On the one hand, we didn't know much about the Philippines other than what Mike had told us—and even that was just vague hyperbole about pretty beaches—so it wasn't like we'd be sacrificing something our hearts were set on. On the other hand, if Sara did indulge Jean in her paranoia and concede to her demands, who could say where it would stop? What if Jean suddenly decided that Indonesia or Thailand was too dangerous, and we had to nix that as well?

The more I thought about it, the more I realized that what really struck me wasn't Jean's reaction, but what Sara had said. She had never rebelled before? *Never?* I thought back to all the ways I'd pissed off my parents when I'd been a teenager: skipping school, missing curfew, taking drugs, getting tattooed. Perhaps the reason Jean was taking her daughter's noncompliance so hard was because it had never happened before.

Sara waffled for a little while, but within a couple of days, she'd made a decision. Officially, it was because our time in Vietnam had been a tad underwhelming and she craved the thrill and grit of a truly unique experience. But I suspected that underneath, it was an assertion of autonomy—that by defying her mother's wishes (which were entirely based on fear) she was making a demand to be respected as an adult.

"Look at you, Miss Girl-Scout-Gone-Rogue," I teased as we searched for flights online.

"Just book the tickets before I change my mind."

I grinned, intrigued by Sara's new rebellious side. Now that she'd had a taste of defiance, who knew where it would lead us? Southeast Asia had suddenly gotten a lot more interesting.

GETTING TO BORACAY wasn't easy. We took a night flight from Ho Chi Minh to Manila, but the turbulence was so bad we couldn't sleep. I spent most of the time white-knuckling the armrest with eyeballs the size of peaches. Sara watched cartoons. Once we arrived in Manila, we boarded something resembling a flying go-kart and, after a second gut-wrenching flight, screeched to a halt on what was less of a landing strip and more of a cross between a thatch of pubic hair and somebody's front lawn.

When we climbed into the tuk-tuk, I leaned my head against my backpack and allowed my eyelids to droop. I'd hoped that all this time spent in transit would have taught me how to survive on less sleep, but now I just prayed that my tan kept up with the dark circles under my eyes. I was just beginning to doze when the tuk-tuk's wheels struck sand and I was practically catapulted back to Vietnam.

"Oh my god, Sue! Look at that!"

It was the most beautiful beach I'd ever seen—so lovely that I was about to say it was probably Photoshopped before I caught myself. The sand looked like it was made of sugar and the water was a playful shade of turquoise, with whitecaps like bubble bath foam. Not a single coconut hung out of place.

"This has got to be the most gorgeous beach in the world," said Sara as we checked into our guesthouse.

"I know! I just want to lie on the sand and, like . . . *be*."

"Amit-ji would be proud to hear you say that."

Laughing, we vowed to spend the entire afternoon soaking up the sun after an hour or two of napping. But when we awoke, it was dark.

"What time is it?" Sara yawned.

I checked my watch. "Eight thirty."

"Oops. Guess the beach will have to wait until tomorrow. Let's grab some dinner, I'm starving!"

We got dressed and headed out. As we neared the sand, we saw flashes of light twisting and dancing in the darkness. At first I thought they were fireworks, but when we got closer we realized that they were actually fire-twirlers. Men with hair down to their waists and tattoos snaking over their shoulders tossed blazing staffs high in the air. Bodacious ladyboys rivaling Vegas showgirls for glitter and panache spun *poi*—twin chains with burning tennis balls at the end—while fluttering their eyelashes and shaking what their mommas didn't give them. The white-hot flames writhed like dragons while club anthems pumped out of the neighboring bars.

"Hey Rasta girl! I like your hair!" called one of the performers.

"Thanks! I like your staff!"

"All the ladies like my staff." He winked, and I blushed feverishly.

We chose a bar at random. After ordering pizza and cocktails, we sat back to watch the fire-twirlers perform incredible stunts as well as some pretty wild dance moves.

"Hola sexy chicas!" A ladyboy who could have been a centerfold, even with her Adam's apple, shimmied over to us, swinging her poi like a lasso. "Where you from?"

"Canada," I said as Sara dropped a coin into the bowl that was discreetly placed on our table.

"That's cool. Welcome to Boracay! We love pretty girls here."

We kept drinking, the fire-twirlers kept flirting, and the music kept pounding so hard that I could feel the bass vibrating in my chest. Finally, we could no longer fight the funk—we skipped over to the dance floor, where locals and backpackers gyrated and writhed and the air was steaming with pheromones. Suddenly, tequila shots floated in front of our faces, held by disembodied hands. And then I was busting out my best moves on the tabletops while Sara grabbed a drink with some blond guy. And then I was making out with a fire-twirler who had a teardrop tattooed on his cheek. And then the line for the bathroom was too long so I decided to pee in the sea—where I promptly fell in and nearly drowned. And then Sara decided it was time to go and so we staggered back to our guesthouse, stumbling into palm trees and losing our flip-flops.

And *then* I was throwing up all of the alcohol, followed by the pizza I'd had for dinner, the pho I'd eaten last week, the cake from my fifteenth birthday, and the button I'd swallowed when I was two. I sagged against the bathroom tiles like an empty pile of skin while the walls whirled around me like a flaming poi ball.

And then I woke up with the worst hangover of my life.

"Come on, Sue, let's go! We have to see a guy about a boat." Sara shook me.

"I think what you mean is, you have to see a man about a horse. And you can go right ahead, although I apologize for the state of the bathroom."

"No, we're supposed to be meeting Robert the pirate! I introduced you guys last night. Don't you remember?"

"You're lucky I remember who *you* are." I groaned and pulled the blanket over my head. "Fuck, it's bright. Would you please turn down the sun?"

"You know how we said we were going to get off the beaten path and seek out weird things? Here's our first chance. Now get up—and for heaven's sake, find some pants. I think you left yours in the ocean."

I downed a handful of aspirin and sought refuge behind my sunglasses. As I lurched reluctantly after Sara, I was craving nothing more than shade, sleep, and a new skull, as this one seemed to no longer fit.

We found Robert at the same bar we'd started at (only now the fire-twirlers were gone, and the table was laden with eggs and toast instead of gin and tonics). He was from England, with sea-salted blond hair and a rich tan. When the sun caught his blue eyes, they sparkled just like the ocean. I nodded hello, then collapsed onto the sand and waited for death.

"Somebody had fun last night." Robert grinned at me.

"Ugh," was all I could reply.

"So, tell me about your boat," said Sara.

"Right. Well, we just finished building it and are ready to set sail. The plan is to turn it into something like a floating hostel. We'll pick up backpackers and then just cruise around for a few days, snorkeling and partying and whatnot. We have to figure out how much it'll be for fuel and food, and then charge people accordingly." He paused to shove a forkful of sausage into his mouth. "At the moment, we're getting ready to head up to Palawan for a few weeks and we're looking for anybody who wants to join us."

"That sounds incredible!" Sara squealed.

"Thanks. You girls want to see the boat?"

He had paddled to shore in a canoe, and as we lolled back out over the waves my stomach felt like a jack-in-the-box, ready to spring up at any moment. Robert's boat turned out to be small but clean—four bunks below deck and two more stacked in the galley—and it was fitted with outriggers. As soon as we docked, a girl, a guy, and two small dogs came to greet us.

"Hi there! I'm Kasey, Robert's sister. This is our friend Kyle."

Kasey helped us aboard and then set to making drinks while we stretched out on the deck. Sara spoke to Robert as I curled up in whatever shade I could find.

"What made you guys decide to do this?" Sara asked. "It sounds like you had a midlife crisis at the age of twenty-five."

Robert laughed. "Something like that. I've always loved sailing and the ocean. Having a boat is the epitome of freedom," he said. "Whenever we get to a place that looks interesting, we drop anchor and head to shore. Kasey has got all the guidebooks for Southeast Asia, although I prefer to explore at random. There are over seven thousand islands in the Philippine archipelago, and the majority of them are deserted. You never know what you're going to find."

"Holy cow, you guys are living the life." A wistful tone lingered in her voice. "But how on earth did you afford to build a boat?"

"Applied to uni, took out student loans, then fled the country. Hang on a tic, let me see if Kasey needs help carrying those beverages." He got up and went to check on his sister.

"He must to be joking," whispered Sara, more to herself than to me. "Nobody is *that* cool."

Robert and Kasey returned with the drinks, and I couldn't bear to even look at mine. The bobbing of the boat was gentle but in my frail state it reminded me all too well of the vomiting free-for-all during our shark-diving experience. I firmly ordered my nausea to subside. After all, puking all over somebody's boat was no way to make friends.

"We're taking off tomorrow for Coron. Apparently there are some shipwrecks nearby that are shallow enough to snorkel," said Kasey. "What do you girls think? Would you like to come along?"

"For sure!" cried Sara without even a glance in my direction. "Definitely. Absolutely. I wouldn't miss it for the world."

"Cool," said Robert. "Listen, I have to pick up some fuel and Kasey needs to go grocery shopping, so we'll drop you off now. You can meet us back at the beach tomorrow morning at ten o'clock."

We climbed back into the canoe, and Robert and Kasey paddled us to shore. There was nary a cloud in sight and the sun was brutal. Dizzy and faint, I splashed some seawater onto my face, but it didn't help.

"Isn't that the most awesome thing *ever*?" exclaimed Sara when we waved good-bye to our new friends and started walking back to the guesthouse. "I can't believe this is their lives! They just gave society the finger and then ran away to paradise. I mean . . . like . . . can they *do* that?" She paused. "Could you imagine if I just called my mother up and told her I wasn't coming home? That I was staying in the Philippines and becoming a pirate? What do you think her reaction would be?"

I leaned over suddenly and threw up behind a palm tree.

"Well, that was an accurate impression," said Sara as I spat and wiped my mouth on the back of my hand.

THE FOLLOWING DAY, we met with Robert as promised. He had also recruited a young Scottish couple named Lena and Derek. Despite nearly sinking the canoe with the weight of our backpacks, we managed to clamber aboard the boat without any impromptu swimming. Then, Kyle raised the anchor and we set sail.

I recalled Mike's description of the Philippines and concluded that even his rhapsodizing had failed to translate its beauty. The ocean was brilliantly teal, with waves glittering like the sequins on a ladyboy's miniskirt. Limestone karsts rose high in the distance, with faces like a thousand knives and plateaus topped with flourishing greenery. Schools of flying fish leaped alongside the boat, skimming the surface for about a hundred feet in a fantastic defiance of gravity before slicing back again into the depths. Of course, there was the occasional Darwinian exception that misjudged the direction and smacked into the side of the boat. But hey, every school has a class dud.

That night, we docked near an arbitrary island and paddled to the beach in the canoe. While the dogs ran off their sea legs, we gathered driftwood for a bonfire. Kasey prepared seasoned potatoes, red peppers, and chunks of eggplant wrapped in tinfoil. As our dinner roasted, night rolled in over the sea on billowing clouds of violet.

"Now be serious. Did you guys *actually* fund this whole thing on student loans?" Sara asked as Kasey nudged her cooking with a stick.

"Not the *whole* thing," Kasey replied, and Sara smiled in relief that such a beautiful fantasy couldn't possibly be true. "I also fly to California for a couple of months every year to work in the Emerald Triangle as a trimmer. But hopefully once things get going, the boat will pay for itself. I know Rob has these grand ideas of making a fortune off this, but I'd be happy if it was just sustainable enough for us to keep going."

"Do you think you're going to do this forever?" I asked.

"Rob might—he's the sailor of the family. Me, I'd like to open up a real hostel somewhere. Maybe in Belize."

For a second it looked as though Sara's eyes were literally burning with envy. But it was just the firelight reflecting off her pupils.

After dinner, Robert reached into the canoe and procured a staff like the ones we'd seen on the beach in Boracay.

"You're not a fire-twirler!" cried Lena. "Are you?"

"Eh, I'm working on the twirling bit. But I can blow a mean fireball." He rinsed his mouth with cooking oil, took a swig of kerosene, and then lit one end of the staff.

"The trick is to spray the kerosene through your lips like you're blowing a raspberry," explained Kyle. "You have to really give it some force, though, or else you'll lose your eyebrows. And remember, it's the opposite of a blow job: it's better if you *don't* swallow."

Robert spat and a gigantic flame whooshed up into the night.

"Holy Mary, he's like Dhalsim from *Street Fighter*!" cried Derek. "I'm next! Lena, did you bring the camera?"

We practiced our fireballs until the kerosene made us sick and we retched into the sand. Upon returning to the boat, I immediately collapsed onto my bunk. Sara, however, set to clumsily wrangling her mattress up onto the deck

"Taking your mattress for a walk?" I inquired.

"The stars are great tonight," she said, blushing at her own mawkishness.

"I don't know about you, but I tend to sleep with my eyes closed."

"Yeah, but . . . oh, Sue, it's all so amazing that I don't want to miss a single thing!"

The next morning, I awoke to a foreboding rumble in my gut. I wasn't sure if it had been the kerosene or Kasey's potatoes, but I had an impending need to suddenly—and probably violently—take a crap. This, however, posed a serious problem. The toilet facilities on the boat couldn't handle anything more solid than urine, so Robert had insisted we take our craps elsewhere, so to speak.

I crept out of my bunk and onto the deck, blinking in the cool morning sunlight. Sara was curled up on her mattress and Robert was splayed and snoring on the deck beside her. I looked around and contemplated my options. We were over a hundred yards from shore, which was way too far to swim. My stomach gave another warning grouse—fuck, I needed to move *fast*. If puking on somebody's boat was no way to make friends, shitting on somebody's boat was likely to get me abandoned on a deserted island.

Without a moment to lose, I pulled on my swimsuit and then dove over the side of the boat. While my colon seized, I picked an arbitrary direction and swam as fast as I could. Goddammit, what did Kasey *do* to those potatoes? When I got far away enough that anybody standing on deck wouldn't see what I was up to, I yanked off my bottoms, aimed downwards, and . . . *man, this is so fucking gross . . . Ew! Ew-ew-ew—oh dear Jesus it's floating back at me!*

I dog paddled away from my shame and back to the boat—horrified that I'd just dropped a deuce in Davy Jones's locker.

"Fancy a morning swim, did you?" said Kyle as I hauled myself back on deck. "You've returned just in time to turn around. Rob checked his GPS and—believe it or not—we're right near that shipwreck! So we're going to go see if we can spot it."

In my absence, everybody had woken up and was now pulling on flippers and snorkels.

"Uh . . . isn't it better to go after breakfast?" I stalled, wondering how long it would take for the evidence to sink.

"Nah, because Kasey's making a big fry-up and we're going to want to digest for a while. Besides, this is so exciting—who wants to wait?"

"Come on, Sue! A *shipwreck!*" squealed Sara. "We'll be like *mermaids!*"

"All right, lads! Into the dugget, as the pirates would say!" called Derek as he flipper-flopped overboard.

My nugget's in that dugget! I thought with alarm. But everyone was splashing down into the water, so I grabbed the remaining mask and fins and jumped in after them. Robert was already leagues ahead, leading the group directly toward the scene of the crime.

"Isn't this terrific?" muffled Sara through her snorkel. "Who knows what we're going to find!"

"Could be anything," I muffled back. "And I mean *anything.* A sunken ship, buried treasure, or just a floating piece of—"

"*Shit!*" yelled Kasey.

My face began to burn. "I just came out for a swim, that's all!" I cried in defense. "Just a regular, run-of-the-mill morning dip! I don't know *what* you think you're accusing me of, but I assure you that it could have been *anybody* who—"

"Sue, what are you on about? I just got stung by a jellyfish,"

Kasey grimaced. "It's not bad, though. Sort of feels like being snapped with an elastic band. Oi! Heads up for the jellies, mates!"

Jellyfish? I ducked under the water to check it out. At first I couldn't see anything, but then movement caught my eye. Pink and ghostly, it was the size of an apple and trailing six-foot tentacles like bicycle streamers. It undulated with a gentle pulse, an elegant expanding and contracting in a rhythm perfectly synchronized with the heartbeat that rushed in my ears. *Ebb and flow . . .*

I surfaced. "Sara! Did you see the jellyfish? It was so cool! Sara?"

"*Sue!*" She was up ahead with Robert and cupped her hands to call back to me. "We found the shipwreck! *You gotta see this!*"

The shallowest part of the wreck was at a depth of only sixteen feet, although the rest sank away into the blurry brine. Soft corals swayed in the gentle current like Muppet hair—Jim Henson's dream made reality. Hard corals bloomed in the shape of trees and mushrooms and brains in every Crayola shade, from Neon Carrot to Screamin' Green. Little fish darted in and out of the crevices, peering curiously at us from beneath the coral shelves. I dove until my ears shrieked from the pressure, captivated by what had once been a rusting hunk of metal and was now a vibrant ecosystem.

"Whoa," said Lena as we tread water to catch our breath. "I don't even . . . I can't even . . . just, *whoa.*"

"So does this count as off the beaten path?" I asked Sara.

"I never want to see that beaten path again!" she exclaimed, and everybody laughed.

"I hear you," said Derek. "I've no idea how I'm going to go back to real life after this."

Robert shook his head. "This *is* real life, mate. This is as real as it gets: not worrying about anything beyond the moment. Everything you do back home—nine-to-five, the rat race, whatever—that's just waiting for real life to begin. And for some people, it never does."

These were the wise words of an inveterate wanderer. I tried to catch Sara's eye to see if she agreed, but she had already disappeared back under the waves.

AFTER THAT, WE docked briefly in Coron before heading toward El Nido, exploring secret lagoons along the way. Some were water-filled caverns so deep that staring down along the rock wall instilled in me a bizarre sense of vertigo, as though I were standing at the edge of a cliff. Others housed tiny cleaner shrimp that nibbled at the dead skin on our toes, tickling and pinching us until we couldn't take it anymore and shooed them away. Offshore, we snorkeled along spectacular coral reefs where venomous sea snakes wove through the water like gymnasts' ribbons and moray eels leered and snapped at us from the shadows. In the distance, sea turtles soared on the submarine currents like eagles on the wind.

While we were sailing, nobody talked very much. Kyle and Robert took turns steering or sitting on the outriggers and grinning at the maritime oblivion. Kasey cooked and flipped through magazines. Derek and Lena took photos and held hands. Sara read a novel. I attempted to write in my journal but was usually lulled to sleep by the warm sun and the gentle rocking of the deck. It was only in the evening that we perked up and really got to know one another.

"What's that tattoo on your arm? Is that the Jolly Roger?" Derek asked Kyle as we sat around the bonfire.

"Yep. I've got a swallow too, although you're not technically supposed to get one until you've sailed five thousand nautical miles."

"What about that scar? It looks like the letter P," said Lena.

"It is. Stands for pirate. Did it myself with a kitchen knife," he laughed. "Might've been a wee bit high at the time."

Sara tilted her head to read the tattoo on his wrist. "Who's Anna?"

"Ex-girlfriend."

"Ouch." Derek winced. "That's why you never ink a lady's name."

"Oh, we'd already broken up when I did it. I've also got her wisdom tooth on a string in the boat somewhere."

Sara and I exchanged glances and simultaneously decided not to ask follow-up questions. Some days we wondered how these guys had so easily rejected the status quo in favor of a nomadic life on the South China Sea. Other days . . . not so much.

In El Nido, we parted ways with Derek and Lena. Their vacation time was nearing an end and they had to return to real life—or unreal life, according to Robert. The following afternoon, Sara, Kasey, and I were sunning ourselves on the deck when Kyle brought word from shore that Robert had found somebody to take Lena and Derek's bunk.

"He's a *dude*," he said, making a face.

"What do you mean, he's a dude?" asked Kasey. "Aren't you a dude?"

"No. I'm a guy. A lad, perhaps. This kid's a *dude*."

Later that day, Robert and our mysterious new guest arrived. As he boarded the boat, Sara's hand fluttered to her chest and Kasey and I high-fived behind a magazine. He was a dude, all right. His shoulder-length hair was blonder and silkier than any of the safari Barbies'. His skin was the color of peanut butter, and his stomach was so impeccably sculpted it looked like he was smuggling bricks under his skin. And when he smiled, his teeth sparkled so brightly that I practically heard a *ping*.

"What up, amigos?" he said in a voice like Michelangelo from the *Teenage Mutant Ninja Turtles*. "The name's Alex."

"Abdominal Alex," I whispered, and Sara nodded in agreement.

"Welcome aboard," Kasey winked coyly. "Where did you say you were from?"

"So-Cal. Yo, you guys don't by any chance know where I can catch some waves in this country, do ya?"

"*Fucking dude*," Kyle mouthed to Robert. Regret dawned on our captain's face as his eyes flicked between Abdominal Alex beaming and the rest of us swooning.

"This boat is rad—thanks, babe," said Abdominal Alex as Kasey handed him a drink. "Mega kudos for letting me join the fiesta."

"No problem," said Robert through gritted teeth. "By the way, there are no *waves* in Palawan. Now, if you'll excuse me, I'm going to go drive this boat. That I built. From scratch." Then he vanished into the helm and I didn't see him again until suppertime.

From El Nido, we made for Puerto Princesa—and it was here we encountered a storm that wracked our little boat with a violent fury. Diabolical clouds loomed overhead, and the ocean turned steely and unforgiving. The winds howled and mercilessly battered the sail as sideways rain worked its way into every crack and cranny. The dogs whizzed back and forth across the rain-soaked deck until Kasey finally bundled them into the galley. We all scrambled to secure ourselves before we were pitched into the thrashing waves.

I sought refuge below deck, where I found Sara lying on her bunk with a woeful expression.

"What's up?" I asked as I crawled into bed.

"Just thinking."

"Sounds dangerous. What about?"

"Robert and Kasey. It's like . . . they did *everything* we're told not to, you know? They didn't try hard in school or save up for the future. Instead, they borrowed from student aid and worked on a grow-op, and here they are living a life that the rest of us can only dream about." She sighed. "I just can't help but wonder if *they're* actually the ones who've gotten it right, and it's the people with jobs who are the idiots."

"You know, Kyle did say he was going to head home in a couple of months. And with Kasey gone to California . . . If you love this boat so much, why don't you come back here? I bet Rob would be happy to have you. You could cook for the other backpackers, and I'm sure he would teach you the basics of sailing."

She shook her head. "You don't understand," she said heavily. "I've got a career waiting for me—one that I've dedicated years of my life to working toward. I can't just *bail*. You're the lucky one; you're only a waitress. There's nothing holding you back. Once you save up some cash, you're as free as you want to be."

I'm the lucky one? I opened my mouth to protest but was cut off by Abdominal Alex poking his head into the room.

"Sorry to interrupt, ladies," he said. "I thought you'd like to know that we have some visitors."

"Visitors? What are you talking about?" I asked, but he just smiled and disappeared from view. Sara and I looked at one another and shrugged. We climbed up onto the deck to investigate.

The storm was over—in fact, both the sea and the sky were so calm, it was like it'd never occurred in the first place. Now, four dolphins raced along just beyond our outriggers. We gasped and clapped as they leaped high into the air, squeaking gaily.

"Look! There's more in the distance." Abdominal Alex put one hand on my waist as he pointed to the horizon where the rest of the pack was frolicking. "That one just did a backflip! Did you see it?"

"I did!" We grinned at each other. There was that *ping* again, and I made a mental note to ask what sort of toothpaste he used. Or if his grandfather had been a disco ball.

The stress of the storm must've exhausted us, as our bonfire that evening was comparatively subdued. After dinner, we reclined silently in the sand, each wading through our own cloistered thoughts as the firelight bounced in our eyes. I could see the muscles in Sara's jaw twitching slightly and assumed she was thinking about Kasey's and Rob's choice of lifestyle in contrast to her own. Although they had shied away from societal tradition, it wasn't like they were slackers picking their nits while life whooshed past. Actually, it was quite the opposite. They had formulated a plan (with a few legally questionable components) and were on the cusp of realizing one hell of an entrepreneurial dream. Even if playing pirate wasn't sustainable forever, Kasey's future hostel could be. Regardless, these siblings had redefined success to cater to their passions as opposed to the other way around.

I could tell by Sara's sudden increase in nail biting that she was rattled by their radical tactics. For the first time since her anguish over deciding whether to do her fourth-grade project on cats or manatees, I saw her being unsure of herself—and that in turn rattled *me*. Perhaps I was looking for answers in the wrong places. Not that I had any desire to sail a boat or run a hostel, but there was something about how Kasey and Robert had so cavalierly changed the meaning of accomplishment . . .

"I don't know about you guys, but I'm falling asleep," yawned Kyle.

"You're not the only one." Kasey gestured to where Abdominal Alex lay snoring. "Let's head back to the boat."

Rob extinguished the fire and the ideas that had begun to flicker ambiguously in the recesses of my mind were startled into smoke.

OUR ARRIVAL IN Puerto Princesa was bittersweet. In many ways, I was going to miss life aboard the boat. The sea life had been so exquisite, the reefs so pristine. My heart sank as I relinquished my snorkel. However, there were certain comforts that I was relieved to indulge in once again. There had been a few more regretful aqua-poos—none quite as nerve-wracking as the first, but still something I couldn't imagine getting used to. Also, no matter how hard we tried to keep clean, any nick or scratch we contracted rapidly became septic in the boat's damp conditions.

Honestly, I was ready to move on and meet some new faces. Our new friends had been great, and we'd had a blast together, but three weeks on a boat with anybody would be a little trying. Of course, there was one person that I regretted leaving. What could I say? He had me at *ping*. But at least he would be joining me and Sara on the flight back to Manila. It would give us some time to get to know each other better. Or something like that.

"Well, that was a crazy couple of weeks," I said as we lined up with our boarding passes.

"Yeah," agreed Abdominal Alex. "That was way gnarly."

"*Way* gnarly," I echoed.

Sara rolled her eyes. "Oh, get a room."

There hadn't been any assigned seats on the plane so the three of us headed to the very last row—cool kids always sit at the back. Sara pulled up the hood of her sweatshirt and popped in her earbuds, and within minutes a light strand of drool was dangling from her lip.

"We're right next to the bathrooms. Guess we'll see if anybody joins the mile-high club," I joked.

"You and I should join the mile-high club," replied Abdominal Alex, and we laughed. *Ping.*

"I bet we could do it if we went as soon as the seatbelt sign switched off," I said. "Theoretically speaking, of course."

"It'd have to be super fast. No points for flash. And it definitely wouldn't be a fair representation of my capabilities, so no judgment." He paused. "Theoretically speaking."

"Of course."

The plane jittered and made a grinding sound as it sped along the tarmac. The wheels lifted and there was that brief yet terrifying moment when my stomach floated in antigravity. Then we began to climb. Through the window, I could see stretches of palm trees and the glimmering sea, green in the shallows and deep sapphire where the land dropped away. The PA system crackled with safety procedures in Tagalog followed by English. Abdominal Alex's hand dangled off the armrest between us, his fingers ever so delicately brushing against my thigh. My breath caught in my throat.

The seatbelt sign flicked off.

Without a word, he got up and stepped into the bathroom, sliding the door closed but leaving the lock ajar. My heart thundered in my chest as my inner monologue shrieked in alarm. Were we *actually* doing this? What if we got caught? What if they deported us? Actually, that wouldn't be so bad since we were trying to leave anyway. Maybe they would just stamp "SLUT" in my passport and call it a day. Or maybe they would throw us in jail and—

While my brain was distracted by paranoia, my body slipped out of the seat and into the bathroom. Abdominal Alex grabbed me by the hair and pulled me into a wet kiss, pressing his tongue fervently against mine and biting down on my lower lip. He slid his hand under my shirt and traced the curve of my side before grabbing my breast. Then, he bent me over the toilet and yanked my shorts down to my knees. I watched our reflections in the mirror as he took me from behind.

"Just for the record, if we were on an actual date this would all be happening way slower," he panted between thrusts. "It'd be really sensual and I'd definitely go down—"

"I get it, Alex! No worries. I promise you'll get rave reviews."

He finished and zipped up his boardies, pausing to steal one more lasciviously sloppy kiss. Then he was gone. I pulled up my shorts, splashed my flushed cheeks, and took a deep breath before stepping out of the bathroom . . .

. . . to be met by the crossed arms and menacing glare of a seriously pissed-off flight attendant.

Panicked, I began to babble. "I am so sorry—I get really queasy on planes—my friend was holding my hair back—please don't call my mother—"

"*Sit down*," Abdominal Alex hissed through clenched teeth.

I sat. The flight attendant eyed us for another moment before deciding she wasn't paid enough to deal with this and returning to preparing the beverage cart. Abdominal Alex and I exhaled in unison.

Sara yawned and pulled out her earbuds. "Did I dream it or did you guys just have sex in the bathroom?"

"We . . . may have."

"Cool." She put her earbuds in again and went back to sleep. Abdominal Alex and I held hands for the rest of the flight.

- 6 -

Smoking Skulls and the Sacrificial Swine

or

Monkey Trouble

AUGUST–SEPTEMBER: INDONESIA

Sara, aboard the longboat: *What do you think is the strangest Western food?*
Local man: *Sandwiches.*

AFTER A LINGERING embrace with Abdominal Alex (under the watchful eye of airport security), Sara and I left Manila for Jakarta, Indonesia. From there we ambled southeast along the island of Java, exploring the colorful streets of Yogyakarta and hiking the smoking crater of Mount Bromo. Then we ferried over to Bali, where the nightclubs blasted Justin Bieber ad nauseam and the touts hawked everything from ice cream to crossbows. Compared with the natural splendor and laid-back attitude of Boracay, rival Kuta Beach felt crowded and garish. However, it did win out in one respect: it was where we met up with Olivia and Aaron, our friends from back home.

They had decided on a trip to Bali last minute and, through Kasey's laptop and the exasperatingly slow Internet connections in El Nido, we'd arranged a rendezvous. Sara and I arrived first and staked out their guestroom. When they trundled in at half-past midnight—glassy-eyed and smelling like airplane—I shrieked so loudly that *shhh* rang out from three separate suites.

"You're so tanned! And blond!" exclaimed Olivia as we jumped up and down.

"Thanks! You're so . . . clean!"

She laughed.

The next few days were spent relaxing in the sand, drinking in the tiki bars, and engaging in an activity that was less like surfing and more like taking the surfboards for a swim. While Sara bargained over souvenirs and Aaron photographed everything in sight, Olivia and I moseyed along the shoreline and caught up on the events of the last seven months.

"All these colors and textures, it was *incredible*," I gushed as our toes sank into the wet sand. "I wish I knew how long that boat had been underwater. Ten years? Fifty years? How fast does coral grow?"

She whistled. "You guys have done *so much*."

"Tell me about it! Africa feels like it was years ago, but it's only been like six months." I paused for a moment of reflection. Then I shook my head. "Sorry, I'm rambling. How are things in Canada?"

"Great! I'm almost done my engineering master's. It's been tough but I know it's going to lead to some incredible opportunities once I start working again."

"Congrats!"

She beamed. "Thanks. Also, Aaron and I are looking into buying a condo in this gentrified area on Queen Street East. It's a bit smaller than we'd like, but really modern and stylish."

"Wow. Things are really coming together for you, eh?"

In the distance, kite surfers leaped over the waves—some soaring majestically while others crashed and splashed into the sea. They reminded me of the flying fish. The sun had already vanished and the tide was beginning to rush out, leaving in its wake tiny shells, sea glass, bottle caps, and seaweed tendrils.

"So I guess you're going to get another waitressing job when you get home, right?"

I shuddered. "I hope not. After everything I'll have done this year . . . how can I go from trekking a mountain to circling a patio?"

"Well, just remember that while conquering ABC *is* an accomplishment, it doesn't make you any more hirable than you were before you left." She lowered the hand that was shading her eyes and looked at me. "Realistically, what other options do you have?"

It was a heavy thought, but she had a point. All of this personal growth wouldn't mean anything to potential employers. *So you went to an ashram—did they give you a diploma? No? Then why don't you check on table six, their chicken is taking a while.*

But then . . . what *was* this trip, anyway? Just a step to the side, moving me neither forward nor backward? Just a brief recess from real or unreal life? It was certainly no engineering master's degree. Or seafaring entrepreneurial venture, for that matter.

"Olivia! You'd better get over here!" called Sara from up ahead. "Aaron's about to buy a crossbow!"

"Oh for the love of—I can't take him anywhere," Olivia muttered, though I could see she was hiding a smile. "Coming!"

We raced across the sand, and the dark clouds of uncertainty brewing over my head evaporated.

WE SOON ABANDONED the gaudy shops of Kuta and headed inland for the flourishing hills of Ubud. As we rolled into town, Aaron read aloud from his guidebook. "It says here that Ubud is the arts-and-culture center of the island. It's home to many traditional dance performances and ancient Balinese temples."

"Hey, is that a Dolce and Gabbana?" asked Olivia.

"*What?* Where?"

"Next to the Ralph Lauren."

Designer clothiers aside, much of Ubud was artistically and spiritually nuanced. There were statues of grimacing demons crouching in the garden corners, and little offerings of rice and blossoms that I kept accidentally stepping on. The four of us explored holy temples where gasping stone faces emerged from the hillsides or peered down from atop ancient doorways. We also sampled *kopi luwak*, a gourmet coffee made from undigested beans collected from the droppings of a weasel-like creature called the palm civet.

Aaron consulted his book again. "Apparently this is some of the most expensive coffee in the world, retailing for up to seven hundred dollars per kilo in the US." He turned to me as I took a swig. "So? How is it?"

I made a face. "It tastes like shit," I said, handing the cup over to Sara.

"Pfft, some people just wouldn't know class if it pooped on them." She sipped it gently. "*Mmm*. Pretension has never been more delicious."

Next, we decided to pay a visit to the Sacred Monkey Forest Sanctuary—a natural reserve home to hundreds of macaque monkeys. The others were excited to go, but I was wary. After encountering the baboons in Botswana, I wasn't sure where I stood on primates. Okay, they were sort of cute, but the memory of their vicious fangs combined with their cunning intelligence instilled within me the heebiest of jeebies.

"Seriously, Sue? You're afraid of *monkeys*?" Sara snorted.

"Just think of them as dexterous babies," suggested Olivia. "Ugly, hairy, dexterous babies."

"And that image doesn't scare you?" I asked incredulously.

She put her arm around my shoulders. "Don't worry, I'll protect you."

"But who will protect *you*?"

"I'm sure I'll be fine."

I remained unconvinced.

The heavy rains of the past few days had kept most of the tourists away. I couldn't decide if that made the Monkey Forest feel serene or eerie. The trees formed a colossal canopy overhead with mossy vines wrapped around their boughs like sleeping snakes. The ground dipped sharply, sinewy roots dangling off the overhangs and pooling in the fissures. The only sounds were the gentle patter of the rain and the dissonant screams of the monkeys. They were smaller than the baboons—only about two feet tall—with wrinkly pink faces and gray fur that was matted from the damp.

"Look! A mother and her baby!" Sara whispered, and Aaron snapped a photo. "Aren't they adorable?"

"Yeah, until they eat your face," I said darkly.

"Come off it. They're more afraid of us than we are of them."

"Speak for yourself."

The macaques didn't seem afraid of us at all. A few of them marched out from the foliage and onto the pavement to size us up like they were preparing to mug us. Which sometimes they were.

"Oi! Cheeky bastard's got my sunnies!" cried one guy as a monkey scampered away with a pair of sunglasses in its mouth, the lenses already cracked. "Those are real Ray-Bans, too!"

Meanwhile, another macaque jumped from a nearby tree and landed on top of some poor lady's head. It perched there with conviction—like the notorious raven atop the door—and none of the snickering onlookers dared attempt to evict it.

"It's okay, sweetie! Just relax!" said her husband, who was undecided between rescuing his beloved and recording a video.

"It's pulling my hair!" the lady squawked.

"One minute they're sitting on your head, the next they're going all *Planet of the Apes* on you," I warned. "And then you'll really be in trouble."

"Have you actually seen *Planet of the Apes*?" asked Aaron.

"No, but I get the gist. Planet full of apes, they're evil and scary, yadda-yadda-yadda."

"That's not what—oh, forget it." Sara shook her head. "That woman is fine. You'd think that after all this time we've spent in nature, you would've calmed down by now. But no, you're just as spazzy as—*eek!*"

She jumped as a tiny beast snapped at her ankles as it scampered past. I crossed my arms smugly.

"Well, *these* monkeys aren't very nice," she admitted. "But maybe this is just a particularly aggressive group. I say we keep going. Give the rest of them a chance. Besides, I haven't gotten any decent pictures yet."

Olivia and Aaron nodded in agreement. I sulked a couple of paces behind the others as we continued farther into the forest. However, after twenty uneventful minutes, it seemed like Sara may have been right. The impudent fiends we'd first encountered appeared to be the exception as opposed to the rule. Most of these monkeys were quite shy, merely eyeing us from the shadows. We saw one juvenile sneak up on another and playfully pull its tail, and we even caught glimpse of a baby that had hardly any fur. I had to confess, it was so hideous that it was almost cute—even though it kind of looked like a hand.

"See? They're not all bad," said Olivia as one of them used a twig to scratch its back in a heart-warming manner. "Here, take this. I'm going to go stand next to that one—you snap a picture."

She handed me her camera and walked over to where a monkey was sitting on the ground, picking at a nut. She turned around and smiled. The monkey looked up.

"Let me just turn on the flash." As I fiddled with the settings, I watched the monkey watching her. Oh lord, what if it . . . *nah.* Sara was probably right—I was just being paranoid. That monkey was only curious. He just wanted to know what she looked like . . . er, smelled like . . . *tasted like!*

Suddenly—and to my indescribable horror—the monkey leaped onto Olivia's leg and bit her in the ass.

"*AAAAAHHHHHH!*" I screamed. "*Heeeeelp!* Monkey attack! Monkey attack! Quick, Olivia! Stop, drop, and roll!"

"What's going on?" Sara and Aaron raced over.

"*She's been bitten!*" Light-headed, I sat down very hard on the path. "Oh my god. Oh my god. What if she, like, catches monkey?"

"It's a macaque, not a zombie." Sara knelt down at Olivia's side to examine the wound. "How does it feel?"

"It hurts, but I think I'm okay. The denim prevented it from breaking the skin." Olivia pulled up the leg of her jean shorts to reveal a mouth-shaped bruise already starting to form, yet—amazingly—no puncture wounds.

"I *knew* this was going to happen!" I wailed. "We've got to get out of here—before they *regroup!*"

Sara rubbed her temples. "Can somebody please shut her up?"

"Actually, Sue might have a point," said Aaron. "I'm sure this was just a fluke, but I'm not keen on pushing our luck. We should go. Besides, Olivia could use some ice."

"Ice sounds like a fantastic idea," Olivia agreed as I leaped to my feet. "Especially if it's floating in a rum and Coke."

And with that, we made our way toward the exit—leaving behind the echoes of screaming monkeys overhead.

A WEEK LATER, Olivia and Aaron were heading home.

"I'll miss you!" I said as I gave her a tight squeeze.

"Aw, don't worry." She patted my back. "The months will go by in a flash. You'll be back home before you know it."

Sara and I exchanged panicked glances. She'd meant well, but her words sent cold shivers down my spine.

With the exception of the monasteries in Tibet and the metropolises in India, our trip had focused predominantly on nature. However, Sara had an anthropological thirst that had yet to be quenched. Which is why, when she discovered an opportunity to visit a traditional longhouse in the backwaters of Borneo, she leaped up with such excitement that she sent the breakfast condiments flying.

"Check it out!" she exclaimed as I rescued the sugar caddy from the floor. "We can *actually* see how the indigenous tribes live!" She thrust down the guidebook and pointed at an entry so brief that a wayward drop of coffee would have obscured it completely.

I looked at it warily. "I don't know . . . it doesn't give much information here. I don't think many people do this."

"*Exactly!*" she cried. "Look, all we have to do is fly to Balikpapan in Borneo, then take a bus to Samarinda, then take a longboat for sixteen hours to Melak—"

"So we're taking a long ride on a longboat to a longhouse? How Freudian."

She ignored my attempt at humor. "Didn't we make a pact to explore off the beaten path?"

"Yeah, yeah. Fine. But if we get sacrificed to the gods, it's your fault."

Sara grinned. "Don't worry, they only sacrifice virgins. You couldn't be safer."

I scowled and returned to my breakfast.

There was one Westerner on our flight from Flores to Borneo—after we lost him in the baggage claim area, we didn't see another for over a week. It took us nearly two days to reach the longhouse, but the journey wasn't without its charm. The longboat meandered north on the Sungai Mahakam, where ambrosial palms dipped their leaves into the river and modest huts teetered above the muddy water on stilts. A taxi then drove us past wet jungles and orchid farms to the longhouse in Eheng.

Like the river huts, the longhouse was also on stilts. Beneath its floors, spring-tailed piglets snuffled after a sow, and chickens pecked and squawked. Despite arriving unannounced, we were greeted jovially by a man with a warm smile and a hearty handshake.

"Welcome! My name is Larry," he said. "It's so wonderful to have visitors again! Tourism has plummeted since the Bali bombings and now we only receive guests about once a year—if that."

After a brief chat, we followed Larry up a ladder made of stripped branches and through the front door. The interior was divided in half—one side featured a series of private rooms that housed immediate family, and the other side was a communal area. Sunlight fell in shafts through cracks in the wooden walls, catching the sparkles of dust and the blue cobwebs of cigarette smoke. Groups of men sat on the floor playing cards, and women sipped tea while babies crawled over their bellies. Children laughed and chased one another while teenagers texted with thumbs a-blur. When they saw us, the adults smiled and the kids pointed and whispered. The teens didn't look up from their phones.

From the ceiling there hung a large box. Decorated with glittering paper cutouts and "god's eyes" (stick crosses bound with colorful yarn), it looked like an elaborate arts and crafts project. I asked Larry what it was for.

"There's recently been a death in the family, and it's customary for celebrations to continue for twenty-one days," he explained. "That box currently holds the remains."

My eyebrows nearly vanished into my hairline. There were *remains* in that box? *Human* remains? Perhaps the longhouse would win me over after all.

The nightly ceremonies kicked off just after sundown. A singer began chanting a low, sorrowful melody into a karaoke machine while a percussionist drummed backup on an instrument made of hanging metal discs. The women and children sat along the walls, and the men lined up single file behind a guy wearing a headdress festooned to match the box. When everybody was in position, he gave a nod and then led the line in a step-two-three-turn type of dance down the length of the longhouse.

Despite what I took to be somber circumstances, the atmosphere of the room was far from serious. The men laughed and chided one another when somebody spun the wrong way, and the singer took occasional breaks from his mournful wails to puff on his cigarette. Meanwhile, the kids were absorbed in a hand-clapping game and paying no attention whatsoever. Soon came time for the women to perform.

That was when a pair of hands grabbed my wrists and yanked me to my feet.

"What the—? Oh, no-no-no . . ." Sara protested as our giggling assailants dragged us into place. My face flushed with nervous excitement, and I couldn't decide whether to laugh or run. I was about to dance in a Dayak death ritual! Could this *get* any wilder?

As it turned out, it could. Before I knew what was happening, the headdress was dropped onto my head and I was shoved past the front of the line. There was a pregnant pause as the entire longhouse stared expectantly at me. Outside, a chicken clucked.

"Oh my god. What do I *do*?" I hissed to Sara through a plastic grin.

"Start dancing!" she hissed back.

"Right. What's the choreography again? Just a jump to the left, and then a step to the right . . . ?"

"You idiot—that's the 'Time Warp'!"

The singing started, and I swallowed hard. Four years of jazz, two years of tap—it all came down to this moment. I took a ginger step forward, another sideways, and then spun around and snapped my fingers. There was a moment of silence. All at once, everybody in the audience burst into hysterical laughter.

"You're doing it totally wrong!" cried Sara as the headdress slipped over my eyes. "What *is* that, even?"

"I don't know! I think I saw it at a bar mitzvah once!"

She shook her head. "This is globalization at its weirdest."

We spent the night at Larry's bungalow next door. The following morning, I awoke to the deafening drum of rain on the tin roof. Sara was still asleep, and I took the moment to reflect on the situation. This was by far the most—pardon the expression—*foreign* experience we'd had to date. We were alone in the backwoods of Indonesian Borneo, surrounded by tribal chants echoing through karaoke machines and human remains stuffed into fancy boxes.

Suddenly, I felt very, very far from home.

Seeing Olivia had reminded me of just how much I missed Toronto, and I'd been daydreaming about eating sandwiches in my mother's kitchen and watching movies in my friends' apartments ever since. They were such mundane fantasies that it was embarrassing to admit them—especially given my surroundings. But I was tired from constantly being on the move. I was lonely with only Sara by my side. Not that I could ever tell her that. She was so stoic—she would never understand. I was already the frightened, whiney, clumsy, clueless one. I didn't want to be the ungrateful brat as well. Perhaps I didn't have it in me to be a career vagabond like Robert and Kasey, after all. But did that seal my fate as a career waitress instead? Our trip was starting to wind down and I was no closer to achieving personal enlightenment than I was when we'd left. Surely all of our ridiculous adventures had meant *something* . . . hadn't they?

Sara woke up an hour later and we discovered breakfast waiting for us.

"I can't wait to see what's going on next door today!" she chirped as she buttered her toast.

"Yeah. Whatever it is, it's going to be cool. Amazing. The time of our lives."

She cocked her head to one side. "Are you okay? You seem a little subdued this morning."

"I'm fine," I lied. "I just didn't sleep very well."

After breakfast, we pulled on our raincoats and headed back to the longhouse. Despite the weather, the activities had been moved outside. A tent had been erected and a red carpet had been laid out underneath. An elderly woman was howling into the karaoke machine and beating her breast in lament—although I suspected her anguish was largely theatrical as she often paused to chitchat with the others.

"Oh my gosh!" Sara was walking ahead of me, and she stopped so abruptly that I smacked into her.

I craned my neck to see over her shoulder. "What is it?"

She stepped to the side so I could have a look. There, arranged on the fabric, were *eight human skulls*. Well, five of them were human skulls. Three of them were coconuts with faces drawn on.

"When someone dies, it's traditional to unbury the heads of the other deceased relatives," explained Larry.

"What are the coconuts for?" asked Sara.

"It takes a few years for the flesh to decompose. The coconuts are stand-ins."

Just then, a man wearing the headdress entered holding a smoldering fern, a twine-bound chicken, a pig wrapped in a tarp—with its curly little tail sticking out—and a spear. He tenderly laid the animals down on the ground and waved the fern above them.

"He's not going to . . . is that chicken a virgin?" I whispered.

The other longhouse inhabitants gathered as he raised the blade high and whispered a prayer. Before I could cover my eyes, he impaled each creature with swift, clean thrusts. The animals wriggled for a few moments before falling still. Their crimson blood pooled in the dirt.

As the sacrifices were being cleaned up, Larry told us that he was heading to Melak and asked if we wanted a ride to the docks. By the time the sun was sinking beyond the river, Sara and I were back aboard the longboat setting sail for Samarinda.

"That was *crazy!*" gushed Sara. "That was like *National Geographic*—our timing was impeccable. We're so lucky!"

"Yeah . . ." I didn't take my eyes off my book.

"Are you all right? You seem off today."

"I'm fine. I'm just tired and missing home." I sighed, then added quickly, "Not that I don't appreciate where we are. It's just . . . we've been going for so *long*, you know? It's exhausting living out of a backpack."

To my surprise, Sara nodded. "I know what you mean. There

are days when I get sick of something as simple as getting lunch being a mission. I miss just being able to go to the fridge." She paused. "I also miss my mother—despite the fact that she drives me nuts sometimes. And my dad. And my cat."

"You do? Why didn't you say anything before?" An accusatory tone crept into my voice.

"What's there to say? The more time you spend pining over what you miss, the more you miss out on what you've got. I find it best to just not think about it."

I couldn't believe it. This entire time I'd been feeling like a wimp, and yet it turned out I'd been comparing myself to a facade. What else had she been putting a brave face on about? Perhaps I wasn't the frightened, whiney, clumsy, clueless one after all!

"All along I've been thinking you were this perfect, unflappable Girl Scout. And yet here you are missing your family—"

She held up her hands. "It's true."

"—and the luxury of convenience—"

"Sometimes, yes."

"—and you were wet and miserable in the Okavango, and cold and drained in the Himalayas, and frustrated and overwhelmed in India—"

"Well, I don't know if I'd go that far."

"—and utterly, cripplingly petrified of the lions and the hippos and the sand fleas and the monkeys and the sharks and the—"

"Good grief, none of *that* stuff ever bothered me. You really do need to harden up, princess!" She laughed as I crossed my arms. "Don't worry, there's still three months left for you to grow a pair."

I scowled and returned to my book.

- 7 -
Ninja Pussy Blow-Dart
and Other Misadventures

SEPTEMBER-DECEMBER: LAOS, CAMBODIA,
THAILAND, SINGAPORE

Sara singing while high on magic mushrooms:
Here a tuk, there a tuk, everywhere a tuk-tuk!

TWO WEEKS AFTER arriving in Borneo, Sara and I were in transit again—this time headed for Laos.

"So this is it," said Sara as our plane taxied on the runway. "Three months left. We're entering the homestretch."

"What? No! I'm not ready for that! I still haven't . . . like . . . *found* myself!"

"Eh." She shrugged. "Wherever you go, there you are."

Something about that struck me as cryptically profound, but before I could give it any more thought, the jet engines roared to life. We were off—leaving behind the animal sacrifices and personified coconuts and touching down amid night markets and riverside bars that could be accessed only by floating down-stream on inner tubes until the bartenders tossed you a rope and reeled you in. Here we discovered the twin tenets of party life for tourists in Southeast Asia: (1) in lieu of glasses, booze is served in the kind of plastic buckets that kids use to make sandcastles and (2) Red Bull contains chemicals way too much fun ever to be approved by the FDA. When mixed with vodka, the effect is not so much to give you wings as it is to fire a rocket up your ass and send you exploding into the night . . . and then crashing into the following morning.

I lifted the damp cloth from my forehead and groaned. "Ugh, pass me the bucket."

"I'm not sure how wise it is that our nights begin and end with buckets," croaked Sara as she handed me the garbage can. "I feel like we're missing out on the Laotian cultural experience."

"We'll start doing the culture thing as soon as we get to Cambodia, I swear." I dry heaved. A strand of spittle dangled from my lower lip. "Besides, I don't know how much more partying

I can handle. I've already thrown up my stomach lining—what happens if I throw up my actual *stomach*, and then my intestines, and then my asshole, and then I flip inside out?"

She wrinkled her nose. "What colorful, yet completely irrational paranoia. Okay, let's make another pact: no more super-crazy-out-of-control-wild nights for the rest of the trip. I didn't come all this way just to leave a trail of vomit across the continent."

"Deal." Wretched and ragged, I collapsed into my pillows and replaced the damp cloth on my face—positive that I would never, ever drink again.

I lasted forty-eight hours.

AFTER A SKETCHY border crossing where various "officials" attempted to relieve us of our "immigration fee" (which probably would've worked had they not been suspiciously cheerful for government employees), we arrived in Siem Reap, Cambodia. Frazzled and sweaty, we each wanted nothing more than to unwind at the bar with a bucket or two. But we stayed true to our word and called it an early night. The next morning, we awoke feeling fresher and brighter than we had since we'd left Borneo.

"I'm so glad we decided on sobriety," said Sara as we sat down to toast and eggs. "Especially since we're visiting the Angkor region today. It was a finalist for the Seven Wonders of the World, you know. Imagine how stupid we'd feel if we tainted the experience with a hangover!"

"I'm just stoked that we're up early enough to order off the breakfast menu," I replied, digging into my omelet. "But yeah, this Wonders of the World place sounds pretty rad, too."

As our bicycle rickshaw went down the dirt road, Sara filled me in on where we were going. Angkor, she explained, was the area in which numerous Hindu and Buddhist temples had been built out of stone by the Khmer Empire between the ninth and fifteenth centuries. What made it unique wasn't just how many temples it comprised, but how architecturally advanced the structures were for their time.

Our first stop was Angkor Wat, which was *gargantuan*. Towers rising almost two hundred feet were arranged in a quincunx, encircled by passages and galleries with corbelled archways and lacey lintels. Elaborate bas-reliefs depicted celestial duels, torturous hellfire, and dancing nymphs with breasts that swelled coyly from the walls. Stairs barely wide enough for a foothold were set at such a daunting incline that they looked like ladders to the world beyond.

"Holy crap!" I sputtered in disbelief. "This place is . . . like . . . totally . . . holy crap!"

Sara laughed. "Did I mention that Angkor Wat is the largest religious structure in the world?"

"How the hell did they build this?"

"Same way they built the pyramids."

"Ah," I nodded in understanding. "Aliens."

"Um . . . I meant, one stone at a time." She gave me a sideways look. "Really, Sue? Aliens?"

Angkor Wat's continued splendor was due to the international funding that ensured its restoration. The other temples in Angkor, however, were much more . . . authentic. And by that I mean I seriously wondered how many tourists were bonked by collapsing rubble each year. For example, the Bayon Temple featured a plethora of stand-alone doorways from which the surrounding walls had long ago disintegrated. The towers were so crumbled and scattered that, from a distance, they just looked like big piles of rock.

"I have to say, this one is less impressive," I commented as we approached. "I'm sure it was awesome in its heyday, but now it's completely dilapidated. After Angkor Wat, it's a bit of a letdown."

"Hang on." Sara grabbed my arm and yanked me to a halt. "Wait for it."

"Wait for what?"

"Just wait."

At first, I didn't understand why we were standing there staring at the temple from afar. But slowly, as if they were actually manifesting before us, the faces emerged. Gigantic carvings with sleepy eyes and gentle lips protruded from all four sides of the towers, vanishing and reappearing with the shadows. The architectural illusion was very effective, evoking the haunting sensation that a supernatural presence did in fact dwell within the ancient ruins. As we explored the temple, we discovered that it was impossible to escape their omnipresent gaze.

"The gods are always watching," Sara whispered.

Despite Bayon's trippy allure, my favorite place was Ta Prohm. In the last few centuries, the surrounding jungle had made a bold encroachment to recapture the holy site. Standing in the center gallery, we gazed up in wonder at the full-sized silk-cotton trees and strangler figs that grew not only *around* the structure, but also *on top* of it. They sprouted from the roof, the sacred pedestal elevating the canopies high above the forest floor. Their roots draped over the doorways like gigantic squid—enveloping and devouring the temple with coiling, sinuous tentacles.

As the bicycle rickshaw took us back into town and the sun vanished into the hazy horizon, I rested my head against the seat and contemplated what we'd seen.

"What's on your mind?" asked Sara.

"I was just thinking . . . When the Khmers constructed Angkor, I bet they never imagined that every day it would be flocked with thousands of tourists from all over the globe. Back then, anybody with the luxury of coming here would've had to undertake a daunting pilgrimage that might've lasted months.

It really *would* have been the experience of a lifetime."

She nodded in agreement. "The advent of air travel certainly has made the world a much smaller place."

"And then I look back on all the incredible things we've done since we left home, and . . . it's kind of a trade-off, isn't it? You always want to see and do as much as you can. But the more experiences you have, the less of an impact each one has on you. Imagine somebody living in the Khmer era who journeyed to Angkor. They would've been filled with such awe and wonder that it would have *literally* changed their life.

"Alternatively," I continued, "Of *course* we thought Angkor was really cool, but the Namibian desert was also really cool, and Annapurna Base Camp was really cool. But 'really cool' isn't necessarily life changing. And, if we hadn't been to any of the other places, Angkor would've seemed that much better." I paused. "It's like we're chasing the dragon."

"Well, I don't like the idea that we're not appreciating what we're doing just because we've had too much of a good thing, but you have a point," Sara admitted. "Everything is relative, and our standard of awesome has been raised to dramatic new heights."

"*Exactly*. Hell, I don't know how we're going be impressed by anything ever again after this year."

"Sheesh, what a depressing thought. That's it—I need a drink."

I snorted. "So much for that pact."

"Hey, *technically* our agreement was no more out-of-control nights. We're still allowed to go to the bar as long as we keep it low-key." She then added in her sternest voice, "Now, Susan, are you capable of behaving yourself?"

I clapped my hand to my cheek in mock offense. "Sara! What do you take me for?"

We both laughed, although I could've sworn I saw a shadow flit across her face.

OUR LOW-KEY, TOTALLY responsible, not-wild-at-all evening commenced at a backpacker bar cutely named Angkor What. When the bartender asked us how we'd like our buckets, we shook our heads and requested one-ounce cocktails instead. *Sara's right, balance is key*, I thought self-righteously. *It's like they say: everything in moderation.*

"Especially moderation," added the English guy standing beside me when I explained to the bartender why I wasn't ordering a pail. He winked slyly, and despite my best efforts I turned the color of freshly chewed bubblegum.

Angkor What's clientele was the usual mix: mainly Britons, a handful of Australians, a few Europeans, the token American who was constantly defending himself against our mostly harmless jabs—and of course two of the awesomest Canadians this side of the Andaman Sea. Backpackers, I'd decided, were the friendliest crowd ever. Maybe because when people were just crossing paths, they didn't have to worry about seeming cool. Or maybe it was because everybody was so sick of their travel buddies that they couldn't wait to talk to someone new. Whatever the reason, everyone was happy and mingling—the giggles getting louder, the dance moves getting raunchier, and the buckets beginning to drain.

"Come on, that's your third one-ounce cocktail! You may as well get a bucket." It was an hour later and we were now sharing a patio table with the English guy, as well as a handful of other buzzing twentysomethings. As more people joined us, we squeezed in to make room—and suddenly I found myself almost in his lap. Not that I was complaining.

"I'm trying to take it easy tonight," I protested good-naturedly. "Don't you peer pressure me!"

"It's not peer pressure, it's fiscal logic. Buying in bulk is cheaper. Trust me, I'm an economist in London."

"You are not!"

"Hey, I could be the King of bloody England for all you know!" We laughed, and he added, "By the way, my name's Riley."

"I'm Sue." I flipped my hair.

"Well, now that we're formally acquainted, allow me to buy you a drink. What's your vice?"

"Vodka/Red Bull. But not in a bucket!"

"Nah-ah-ah. Beggars can't be choosers, darling." There was that wink again—his eyes sparkling like coins in a wishing well— and I found myself blushing for the second time. *He is smoking hot*, I thought as he went up to the bar. *Susunka, you have done well for yourself!* When he returned, it was of course with a bucket (in fire engine red, no less) and it sloshed onto the tabletop as we toasted.

"So, what do you actually do in England?" I asked as I took a sip. Lord, that was *strong*.

"Oi. How about we not have that conversation?" He scratched at his customs-stole-my-razor stubble. "I'm not being rude—it's just that, when I'm on holiday, I try to forget about everything at home. Backpacking is about meeting new people and having new adventures. The last thing I want is my old life trailing behind me and cramping my style, like a bad smell."

"*Riley!*" Without warning, he was interrupted by a beautiful girl with hair like dark chocolate and lashes so long they made a whooshing sound when she blinked. "For fuck's *sake*! Why didn't you leave a *note* as to where you were *going*? I woke up and you were *gone*!"

"And yet you managed to find me," Riley said through gritted teeth. He shuffled over to make room—his hand landing briefly between my thighs—and she sat down on the far side of him, kissing his cheek begrudgingly.

"Of course I found you. This place isn't that big, you know.

I just looked for the bar with the loudest music and the drunkest girls." She flashed me a catty smile. "I'm Robyn, by the way. Riley's *girlfriend*."

"Speaking of your old life cramping your style." It was out of my mouth before I could stop it, and Riley shot me a look. "I mean . . . uh . . . it's nice to meet you. I'm just on my way to the bathroom, I'll be right back." Excusing myself from the table, I caught Sara's eye and gestured with a sharp nod. She got the hint and broke away from the conversation she'd been having with a longhaired beach bum to follow me.

"What's going on?" she asked, eyes alight with the promise of drama. "Who's that guy who bought you the bucket? He is smoking hot, by the way!"

"That would be the boyfriend of the gorgeous chick who just showed up."

Apparently Sara had also been cheating on our everything-in-moderation rule—she was so shocked by this revelation, which didn't concern her in the slightest, she staggered backward and crashed into the sink. "Oh. My. *God*. What are you going to *do*?"

"Absolutely nothing. I'm not getting into that kettle of worms, or . . . whatever," I hiccupped. That bucket was going to my head. "That couple's got issues and I am *not* getting involved. I'm just going to go find the American guy and talk to him. He was nice, wasn't he?"

"He's a Republican."

"*Sara!*" I gasped. "I know we're both drunk, but that's just *rude*!"

We stumbled out of the bathroom and back to the table. Fortunately, somebody had stood up to get another drink and I snagged the vacant seat, avoiding eye contact with Riley and Robyn. As it turned out, the American *was* nice (as long as nobody mentioned Stephen Colbert) and while his eyes didn't quite sparkle like coins in a wishing well, they did look sort of like cookie bits in a glass of milk. Or something like that.

An indiscernible amount of time later, I heard Sara calling my name. When I looked up, I saw her standing by the door with the beach bum and his buddies. "We're going to go dancing at this place on the other side of the road," she said. "You in?"

"Absolutely! Let me just finish my drink, I'll meet you there." Forgoing the straw, I lifted the bucket—which was now blue (when did that happen?)—to my lips and gulped down its contents with the elegance of a pelican gulping down a fish.

"Sue! Slow down before you choke!" Cookie Eyes laughed. "Listen, I have a confession to make: I'm not much of a dancer. But I *am* really enjoying our conversation. Why don't the two of us stay here instead?" He draped his arm across my shoulders in a casual yet optimistic advance.

From where we sat on the patio, I could see Sara and the others scamper tipsily across the road. As they went inside the club, I contemplated his offer. I *was* feeling rather intoxicated—this had the potential to turn into a sloppy night. *Going to a nightclub is not a good idea*, the voice of reason piped up in my head. *Remember how sick you felt after that night in Boracay.*

It was sound advice. But just as I was about to turn back to Cookie Eyes, who should rock up to the club but Riley and Robyn. They paused so Robyn could fix the strap on her sandal, and Riley glanced up . . . and caught my eye. And winked.

"Nah, I really have to go. But you should definitely *stay here.* I mean, since you don't like dancing and all. Anyway, it was nice meeting you! Good luck bringing down Comedy Central!" Before he could respond, I leaped to my feet and hurtled myself over the patio railing—having abruptly forgotten all about the door—and raced across the street.

The nightclub was dark and reeking of sweat and spilled drinks.

The bass was cranked up so high that I could feel the button on my jean shorts vibrating against my lower abdomen. Pushing through the writhing crowd, I tripped over somebody's lost flip-flop and crashed into a chick with hair like dark chocolate.

"Oh my god! Sue!" Robyn had obviously had a few, because she was much happier to see me now than she'd been the first time around. She gave me a big hug and offered me some of her bucket. "By the way, your hair is, like, *amaaaaazing*!" she gushed as she ran her fingers through my dreadlocks. Her face was very close to mine and her lip gloss smelled like maraschino cherries. I hiccupped nervously.

"Ladies!" Riley appeared between us and slid one arm around each of our waists. "It's *excellent* to see the two of you getting along! Why Robbie, you've almost finished your bucket. Why don't I grab another for you girls to share?"

She giggled. "Are you trying to get me drunk?"

"Now why would I ever do that?" He kissed her mouth and grabbed her ass—lifting her skirt so high that I could see her panties sneaking up her bum in that way that's uncomfortable to experience but was so titillating to watch—before vanishing into the crush of the crowd.

Robyn readjusted her dress, her cheeks flushed with alcohol and arousal. "I *loooooove* this song!" she cried. "Let's dance!"

Before I could answer, she dragged me onto the dance floor and pressed her chest so tightly against mine that I could feel our nipples making acquaintances through our tank tops. Her face was very close again—wait, were those maraschino cherries or black cherries?—and the next thing I knew we were hot-and-heavy making out, her tongue so far down my throat that I could almost feel her licking my supper.

"Riley's right, you *are* sexy," she murmured. "I think you should come home with us."

I *knew* this would turn into a sloppy night—what was *in* that Red Bull? I paused to consider my options. On the one hand, I'd never gone home with a couple I'd met only hours before. On the other, it wouldn't be my first threesome, and Riley and Robyn seemed pleasant enough. Not to mention that it'd been quite a while since Abdominal Alex, which had been exciting but somewhat lacking in finesse . . . Ah screw it. What was the worst that could happen?

I kissed her again. "Count me in."

We found Riley, who handed his bucket to the random guy next to him and bustled us out the door and into a tuk-tuk before we changed our minds. As we pulled away from the club, the world continued to pound and spin. Holy hell, I was *plastered.* And, given that Robyn's dress was up around her waist and Riley was no longer wearing any shoes, it was obvious that they were too. But before I could consider the implications of such a situation, Robyn leaned over and bit my neck. Then she leaned over and bit Riley's neck. Then he leaned over to me and—Robyn grabbed him by the hair and reeled him back. "You can't touch her," she slurred.

Ah. I was up to speed.

The rest of the ride was a blur of tickles and strokes. We arrived at the guesthouse and scrambled up the stairs, and the bedroom door hadn't even clicked shut before Robyn stripped to the skivvies. She wasn't quite as hot as I'd thought at first (her areolas were too large and she had a tattoo of a *fairy*, for Christ's sake) but no matter, I was still up for a good time.

I threw off my clothes and shoved her backward onto the bed. She eagerly lifted her hips as I slid off her panties . . . yikes, that was some *major* stubble. Perhaps customs had stolen her razor, too. As I leaned down between her legs, Riley came up behind me and put his hands on my waist—

"*Oi! I said you can't touch her!*" Robyn snapped upward, accidentally cracking me on the nose with her pelvic bone.

"Don't worry, babe," I pushed her back down with one hand and checked if I was bleeding with the other. "I'm here for *you.*"

It wasn't exactly true, but instinct told me that it was prudent to make allies. She smiled graciously at me, and we swapped positions so that she could be the middleman. I lay on my back and closed my eyes, and Robyn's tongue had just begun to flutter and flick when she suddenly stood up.

"I have to pee!" she announced with the shamelessness of a naked drunkard.

She stepped into the bathroom and I looked at Riley, wondering what sort of small talk would be appropriate for the situation. *So, is it safe to assume that your favorite flavor of ice cream is Neapolitan?* Riley, however, had other intentions. No sooner had the bathroom lock snapped into place that he was on me—*in* me—and I admit that, although I did have a pretty good idea of what was coming—no pun intended—I didn't stop him.

"*GET THE FUCK OFF OF HER, YOU FUCKING CUNT!*"

Robyn attacked with the fury of . . . well, with the fury a girl who's just caught her boyfriend banging some other chick, which is powerful enough that we can skip the simile. She punched him in the ribs and barraged him with slaps, screaming, "This is the sixth fucking time you've cheated on me, you fucking asshole!"

Then, as if a switch had been flipped, she abruptly turned to me and apologetically said, "I'm so sorry, darling. It's not you. You're beautiful."

"What the fuck is wrong with you?" Riley snarled as handprints patterned his skin like pink snowflakes. "What did you think was going to happen? It's called a threesome, not a two-and-a-half-some!" And then he also became eerily demure. "Please don't take this personally, Susie. You really are gorgeous." Back to Robyn: "You bipolar cow!"

"You horny twat!"

"Oh no-no-no, it was your horny twat that got us into this!"

Nothing ruins the mood of a three-way like a domestic dispute. I snatched up my clothes and ducked into the hallway with only one leg in my shorts. Racing down the driveway, I could still hear an ominous torrent of shrieks and crashes. When I reached the street I skidded to a halt, still drunk, mostly dressed (I'd lost a flip-flop), with no idea where I was, and—I realized with horror—with no money in my pockets.

Well, now you've done it, lectured the voice of reason. *I'm not going to say I told you so. I'm just going to think it really, really loudly.*

Oh, shut up, I told the voice. *I'm the star of this narrative. Certainly something will come along at the last moment and save me from being murdered in the back-alleys of Siem Reap.*

Sure enough, just then a teenage boy on a motorcycle rode past, pausing to blow me a kiss as local boys often did to Western girls. I frantically flagged him down, hoping that my damsel-in-distress-ness would outweigh my shoeless-alcoholic-ness.

The teen pulled over and I jumped on the back of his bike. "I'm sorry, I don't have any money," I said after telling him the name of my guesthouse. "Please don't rape and/or kill me."

He stared at me blankly for a moment before gunning the engine. The motorcycle lunged at the road ahead faster than an irate girlfriend at a cheating scumbag, and I had to grab his waist to keep from flying off. When we arrived at my guesthouse, I gave him a peck on the cheek in gratitude.

"Thank you *so* much!" I said as a blush spread across his face like wildfire.

Amid the chaos, I had somehow managed to hang onto my

room key. I let myself in and discovered Sara brushing her teeth.

"Wah happah?" she asked through a mouthful of toothpaste. "Whed yuh goh?"

"There was a bit of a communication breakdown between Riley and Robyn." I recapped the night and she gaped at me with toothpaste dribbling down her chin. "But they ended up turning on each other instead of on me. Which was fortunate, because from the looks of it, Robyn's got a mean left hook."

Sara laughed and shook her head. "Wow. I don't know how you get yourself into these situations, Sue."

"I do. It's called alcohol."

"Which is all the more reason for us to re-enact our pact. No more super-crazy-out-of-control-wild nights for the rest of the trip." She stood up and returned to the bathroom. "And this time *I really mean it.*"

"And miss out on more nights like this? Sorry, Sara, but not on your *life.*"

FROM SIEM REAP, Sara and I bussed to the beachside town of Sihanoukville. We arrived at our guesthouse just after sunset, when the lapping ocean waves reflected lilac and periwinkle. After dropping our bags in our rooms, we headed downstairs to the guesthouse bar and pulled up a couple of stools, nodding hello to the other backpackers. As the bartender was preparing our buckets, three of his coworkers snuck up behind him and burst into off-key singing while brandishing a birthday cake. Grinning sheepishly, he blew out his candles, and everyone clapped as the cake was cut and distributed.

"Oh, I wonder what's in this!" I said to the guy in the pageboy cap next to me as I was handed a slice.

He looked at me, then looked at the cake, then started to grin. "I don't know," he said, a little too innocently. "Why don't you tell me?" And then he snatched the slice right off my plate and *smashed it into my face.*

"Oh no you *didn't!*"

I grabbed his piece and whipped it at him in retaliation— although my aim was severely compromised by the dollop of icing melting into my eye. The cake sailed way off course and smacked into the side of some girl's head. "*Food fight!*"

Strawberries flew through the air like grenades. Ladyfinger cookies were crammed up noses. The staff members were power- less against the crazy *falangs*—not that they were trying that hard to stop us. I noticed the bartender seize his opportunity and dump half the cake on his boss's head, which must have made it a very happy birthday indeed. When we finally ran out of dessert to throw, we all raised our glasses in a sticky, laughing round of cheers.

"And on that note, my name is Paul." The guy who'd started the fiasco tipped his cap to us. "From Ireland."

His friends—who were English—introduced themselves as Wally, Cheryl, and Rudolph. Wally was handsome in the boy-band way and his girlfriend, Cheryl, was petite and perky. Rudolph, on the other hand, was a hulking individual covered in tattoos that were equal parts erotic and ridiculous.

"What do you for a living?" Sara asked him.

"I'm a drug dealer," he answered candidly. "I also do children's parties."

"You also do *what* at children's parties?"

He laughed. "Don't worry, I'm a clown. Want to see a magic trick?"

Without waiting for a response, Rudolph whipped out a pack of cards and prompted me to select one (jack of clubs) and then put it back in the deck. After a series of gravity-defying shuffles, he procured a card. "Is this is it?"

Four of diamonds. "Uh . . . no."

"Shit. How about this one?"

Six of hearts. This was getting awkward. "Nope, sorry."

"What about this?"

"Hey! That's my iPod!" squealed Cheryl.

"Sorry 'bout that, love. Old habits die hard." He winked. "Now, Susie, is that the jack of clubs in your pants, or are you just happy to see me?"

Giving him a sideways look, I reached into my pocket—and felt something that hadn't been there before. "Oh. My. God. It *is* the jack of clubs!"

"I was hoping for the second option," he said to Wally. My cheeks flushed.

We spent half the night captivated by Rudolph's illusions before remembering that we were supposed to be out partying. Once again, we succumbed to a succession of buckets and awoke the next day so hungover that the only thing we were capable of was lying down on the beach. However, that was pretty much all there was to do in Sihanoukville, and so it was with a clear conscience that we ducked behind our sunglasses and collapsed onto the sand.

The beach wasn't as beautiful as those in the Philippines (nowhere was), but the water was cool and refreshing. We dove over the waves and splashed around, drowning our hangovers in sea salt and sunshine. Eventually, Sara, Cheryl, and I climbed out to work on our tans (and perhaps sneak in a four o'clock cocktail) while the boys stayed in, their laughs and whoops echoing down the shoreline.

All of a sudden, a tortured scream ripped through the playful atmosphere. The girls and I raced to where Rudolph and Wally were dragging Paul out of the water. The Irishman was white-faced and gasping. On his thighs were deep, purple gashes already welling with milky pus.

"What *happened?*" cried Cheryl.

"Jellyfish," Rudolph explained grimly. "Look—you can still see it floating over there!"

Sure enough, a white blob the size of a beach ball bobbed in the brine, its short tentacles thick and curled like gnarled fingers. A couple of local men immediately yanked it out and beat it to smithereens with a paddle. Meanwhile, Sara knelt down and examined Paul's wounds.

"He's not critical, but we should get him to a doctor," she said.

"*MOTHERFUCKING FUCK FUCK SHIT!*" yelled Paul. "*SWEET JESUS MERCY OF FUCK!*"

"Is there anything we can do before he passes out from the pain?" asked Wally.

"I-I'm really not familiar with this kind of chemical burn," stammered Sara. "I don't know—does anyone have any suggestions?"

"*ONE OF YOU CUNTS FUCKING PISS ON ME!*"

There was a moment of silence as five sets of eyebrows reached for the heavens.

"Is he, like, delirious or something?" Rudolph asked finally. To Paul, he said, "Don't worry, mate, you're not dying. You don't need to make any weird final demands."

But Cheryl snapped her fingers. "Wait a sec—he's thinking of that episode of *Friends*! Remember the one where Monica gets stung by a jellyfish and Chandler has to pee on her?"

"Oh yeahhhh, I saw that," I said. "Does it actually *work?*"

"Beats me," said Sara. "I can't imagine it'd make it any worse."

"*PLEASE! I'M BEGGING YOU! FUCKING PISS ON ME!*" Paul's eyes rolled back in his head.

"All right, we'll do it!" declared Wally. He turned to Rudolph and nodded expectantly. "Well? Go on then. We haven't got all day."

"*Me?* Why don't *you* fucking do it?"

"*Because!* It's a little . . . sometimes I have . . . *difficulty* . . . when there's an audience!"

"And what makes you think I don't also have . . . *difficulty?*"

They glared at each other with crossed arms and red cheeks.

"Oh for the love of—*move over!*" Cheryl shoved the boys aside. "I'll pee on you, Paulie!" And before anyone could say anything else, she whipped off her bottoms, squatted down, and whizzed all over his oozing legs.

Now, it must be said that, while we had all seen the episode of *Friends*, the hundreds of Cambodian locals on the beach that day had not. And so I could only imagine what was going through their minds as they watched some little white chick piss all over a screaming, bleeding Irishman. Especially since—as we quickly discovered—the remedy was just an old wives' tale. The Irishman continued to scream and bleed, and now he stank quite rudely as well.

It was at that point we decided it would be best to let the medical authorities take over. The boys carried Paul to a tuk-tuk and Sara escorted him to the hospital while the rest of us went back to the guesthouse to wait. I anxiously crossed my fingers. What if Sara had been wrong about the peeing, and we actually *had* made it worse? What if the pee and the sting created some sort of terrible chemical reaction and now . . . now they had to *amputate?* Then he'd be Peg-Leg Paul, and it would be all our fault! Rather, it would be all Sara's and Cheryl's and Wally's fault—for the record, *I* never conceded to *any* of it.

They returned a couple of hours later and I was relieved to see that Paul had all his limbs accounted for. In fact, despite being bandaged and limping, he was in high spirits. The doctors had said he would be fine in a few weeks (though with some nasty scars) as long as he got plenty of rest and didn't party too hearty.

"This calls for a celebration," he grinned. "Barkeep! A round of buckets!"

"I can't believe you're drinking right now. Aren't you on a lot of medication?" asked Wally.

"I can't believe how eager you were for a golden shower," said Rudolph, and Cheryl elbowed him in the ribs.

WE SPENT A few more days in Sihanoukville before the gloomy yet inevitable time came for everyone to part ways. Cheryl and Wally were heading to Australia and Rudolph was flying home. But Paul didn't have any set plans, so we invited him to join us for the Full Moon Party on Koh Pha Ngan. Koh Pha Ngan is an island in Thailand whose economy more or less revolves around the festivities that bring twenty to thirty thousand visitors each month. Although the moon is technically only full for one night, the party rages on for the entire week. Every other building is a bar, and at least three tattoo shops and one clinic are visible from any given street corner.

At night, the beach became a hedonistic playground. Stalls selling booze buckets stretched as far as the eye could see. Deejays blasted the same twelve club anthems on a loop. Fire-twirlers spun not only staffs and poi, but also flaming skipping ropes that the drunken tourists could try their luck at—which could explain the clinics. Bars and hostels supplied fluorescent body paint so everybody had an excuse to tickle one another with paintbrushes. And then there was Paul, who just painted himself neon yellow from head to toe so that Sara and I couldn't pretend to lose him in the crowds when he got too obnoxiously drunk.

The three of us quickly made new friends: a trio of English boys who partied like rock stars from the moment they woke up until they collapsed into bed, or onto the floor, or onto the sand, or wherever else they happened to be when they finally passed out. There was Ben, the tattoo artist who had banged more girls than Ghengis Khan (albeit with a much better track record of mutual consent); Steve, whose young parents had raised him in their college dorm; and Sam, who—through some ghastly glitch in natural law—could lick his own testicles. Ben was a charismatic flirt and Steve was an easygoing joker, and Sam . . . well, Sam was typically naked and staggering.

"I wen' on dish cruish one time, baaaaabe," he slurred with what was either heavy intoxication, a regional accent, or a mild lisp—nobody seemed to know. "An' I got shee legsh, and it, like, never wen' awaaayyy."

It didn't take long for Sam to develop a crush on me. He actually was attractive—or he would've been if his eyes ever opened and if he didn't wake up each morning covered in mysterious wounds that oozed all over the patio chairs—and charming in a piss-off-your-dad sort of way. However, I was still hung up on Rudolph (with whom I'd shared a few sensuous evenings) and thus Sam's persistent advances were in vain. But he was still great fun. In fact, the only real problem with the boys was that Paul, Sara, and I struggled to keep up with their antics. Fortunately, we had help: Thai pharmacies were somewhat lackadaisical in their laws and so we were able to purchase a whole new spectrum of poison-for-pleasure right over the counter.

"What is it that we're buying again?" I asked, stifling a yawn. It was our fourth day on the island and the lifestyle was beginning to catch up with me.

"Dexedrine. Officially it's ADHD medication, but essentially it's speed," explained Sara. "For when Red Bull just doesn't cut it anymore."

"Doesn't this, like, go against your professional ethics or something?"

She shrugged. "Eh. After letting you guys pee into an open sore, I think that's a moot point."

The dexies gave us the edge to finally keep pace with Ben, Steve, and Sam—although our pupils were now the size of dinner plates and we twitched sporadically. That was okay; the only real downside was the sleeplessness. Sara and I managed to compensate with Valium (also available over the counter), but Paul required something more powerful to knock himself out.

"They told me this was the strongest stuff they had," he said as the two of us left the pharmacy. He pulled out the blister pack of tablets and looked it over.

"Let me see that." I grabbed the pack and read the label. "Rohypnol. Holy crap—Paul, these are *roofies!*"

"*No fucking way!*"

I burst out laughing. "Only you would roofie yourself!"

"Jesus, I can't take these! They really fuck you up. What should we do with them?" The words were barely out of his mouth when an all-too-familiar grin spread across his face. I decided not to ask.

The shadows were just beginning to stretch when we arrived at the bar where the others were indulging in pad thai and beer.

"Mished you, baaaaabe," slurred Sam as he gave me a hug. "How's abou' a hello shnog?"

We sat down, and I forgot all about Paul's plan until it was his turn to get the next round, and I went along to help him carry it. Standing at the bar with his back to the table, he popped out one of the Rohypnol pills, crushed it between his fingers, and dropped the powdery crumbs into Sam's beer.

"Are you spiking your friend's drink with Viagra?" the bartender asked (which likewise could be purchased without a prescription).

"Of course not! What sort of asshole do you think I am?" cried Paul. "It's a roofie."

The bartender shook his head. "Just make sure he doesn't throw up in my bar."

"Are you sure this is a good idea?" I asked.

"Hey, it'll get him off your back for the night. Besides, I ran it by Ben and Steve and they think it's hilarious. So does Sara." He glanced back at our table. "Are you *sure* she's a nurse?"

We brought the drinks over and Sam downed his without suspicion. For the first forty minutes, nothing happened. Then his head began to droop ever so slightly. Watching him out of the corner of our eyes, we continued to chat as if nothing was awry until he suddenly face-planted into his noodles.

"You all right, mate?" asked Ben as Paul and Steve struggled to maintain their composure.

"Yeah. Jush' really tired for shome reashon." Sam flicked a bit of shrimp out of his moustache. "Nex' round, I'm on to Red Bull."

But he didn't even make it that far. Not ten minutes later, he passed out cold—falling right out of his chair and landing in a bewildered heap on the floor. The bartender gave Paul a quizzical look, but the Irishman didn't notice as he and Steve were doubled over in hysterics.

"Fuck, I'm gettin' a dexshie." Sam pulled himself to his feet, shook his head, and stumbled out onto the road wearing only one flip-flop.

"Where's he off to?" asked Sara.

"He's . . . getting . . . speed," Steve gasped as he wiped a tear from the corner of his eye.

"*What?* You can't let him do that! Slipping him date-rape is one thing, but if he mixes uppers and downers, he could have a heart attack!" she cried.

"*Shit!*" The boys exchanged a terrified look—then raced out the door to catch Sam before he accidentally offed himself.

"'Slipping him date-rape is one thing'?" I cocked an eyebrow at Sara.

"Hey, I didn't see you intervening when Paul dropped it in Sam's glass," she said defensively. "And *don't* say it was my duty because I'm the nurse!"

"Let me get this straight: Sam is out foaming at the mouth somewhere because *you* didn't want to seem like a buzzkill?" I paused. "Fuck, I can see it now: Paul and I are on some daytime talk show, me with prematurely gray hair and him in a prison jumpsuit, and the host is reminding the viewers to talk to their kids about drugs—"

"First of all, Sam will be fine," she snapped. "And secondly, why are you suddenly blaming me for this? What, you think that deeming me the responsible half absolves you of all your stupid decisions? You're not a child, Susan. In fact . . . you're three months older than me!"

I threw my hands up in the air. "Of course. Those twelve weeks I spent shitting black stuff and eating my feet while you were still bathed in placenta should've really given me a leg up in life. Sorry I'm such a slacker."

"You're the one who said it," she mumbled.

"Oh my *god*! You think I'm a *slacker*?"

"Well, if you invested half the time you spend whining about being a waitress into pushing yourself into being anything but a waitress, you wouldn't be a waitress anymore!"

I gasped squeakily. "Easy for you to say, Miss Straight-A Girl Scout!"

"You would've gotten A's too if you'd actually gone to class once in a while. Did it ever occur to you that maybe I wasn't just blessed with vast quantities of knowledge? That maybe I had to work really, really hard to get where I am?" she retorted. "And don't spit 'Girl Scout' at me like it's some sacred standing—you were a Scout for a week before you decided that it was just a way of tricking kids into good behavior and dropped out. What six-year-old thinks like that?"

"It's true! Look how well-behaved you are!"

"Only because when I'm not, people suddenly get roofied!"

The two of us glared at each other with our arms crossed.

"You shouldn't complain about being smart and rational," I said begrudgingly. "I'm sure it comes in handy sometimes."

"I'm not complaining. But you shouldn't allow the fact that you have a crappy job to determine how intelligent you are and justify acting accordingly. If you want to do something with your life, stop overthinking it and getting in your own way—just shut the fuck up and do it!"

After nearly an hour, the boys returned—but it was without Sam. Despite our argument, Sara and I instinctively grabbed for each other's hands.

"It's okay, we found him," said Steve, and we breathed a sigh of relief. "The good news is that he hadn't taken the pill yet. The bad news is that, when we told him what we did, he had a panic attack."

"He *what*?"

"He's got this anxiety problem—he's been on medication for years," explained Ben. "We sort of forgot about that when we decided to roofie him."

"He'll be all right. We left him in the care of these two super-cute Kiwi chicks that promised to kiss it better," Paul winked, and Steve snorted. "He was pretty pissed off, though. Which is why we blamed it on Sue."

"You *what*?"

"He'd kick the shite out of us—he won't get that mad at you!" Paul cried as I lunged at him with a plastic fork.

All jokes aside, we did feel terrible about what we'd done to Sam. Nobody was in the mood for partying on the beach anymore.

The guilt had left a bitter taste in our mouths—although with Paul around, you never knew if that wasn't just a roofie. In any event, we needed a new plan for the evening.

"Perhaps we should just take it easy tonight," suggested Sara. "I mean, we *have* been pushing ourselves to the limit. Our bodies need a break. I haven't emailed my mother in a week, and Sue, how long has it been since you wrote in your journal?"

"She's got a point. Dexedrine or not, I'm *exhausted*," I said, and Paul agreed.

To my surprise, Steve and Ben weren't totally appalled by the notion. "I brought a book that I haven't looked at since the airport," said Steve. "And Ben, weren't you saying you had some tattoo ideas you wanted to sketch out? Maybe having a quiet one *is* a sound plan." He paused. "Or we could just go get happy shakes at the Mushroom Mountain Café. Whatever you guys want."

As its name implied, the café was located on top of a mountain. A narrow staircase with no railings ran steeply up the cliff face, and rocks jutted up from below, waiting—like something out of a video game—to impale a falling body. I wondered how many tripped-out travelers toppled to their death each full moon, and if the location had been chosen out of malicious humor or evolutionary experimentation.

The café itself was comfy and inviting with beanbag chairs and Christmas lights. As its name also implied, it served milkshakes made from magic mushrooms. We bought a round and then built ourselves a nest out of pillows on the patio overlooking the ocean. It was overcast and so the water and sky were a deep slate gray. I watched the orange flames and green strobes dart and dance on the beach amid the partygoers as I downed my shake. It tasted like chocolate and trees.

"I don't think this is doing anything," said Ben after about half an hour. "I'm going to get another one."

"Hey, guys," said Steve. "Do you see that coconut over there? Is it, like . . . *looking* at us?"

I turned to see what Steve was referring to, but became distracted by the Christmas lights that had suddenly begun to hop and quiver.

"My heart's beating really fast." Paul put his hand to his chest. "Oh fuck. I think I'm having a heart attack!"

"Seriously, that coconut is *watching* us! It looks friendly, though. Let's name it Ethel. Oi, Ethel! Come over here!"

"I'm having a heart attack! *I'm having a fucking heart attack!*"

"You're fine," said Sara. "My heart feels the same way."

"You're *having a fucking heart attack!*"

"I can't believe Ethel's ignoring me. What a cunt." Steve paused. "I shouldn't have used that language. Sometimes I forget that words hurt."

"*Is nobody fucking listening to me? Sara and I are having heart*—holy shite, what happened to my legs?"

"You got stung by a jellyfish, remember?" said Sara.

"Oh right. Hey, if you guys don't call it jelly in Canada, would it be a jamfish? Or a marmafish?"

"Like a marmadillo!" cried Steve.

"That's an armadillo," said Ben. "Does anybody else hear a dog barking? Sue? Sue!"

I was too lost in the patterns of dancing lights to reply. The colors swished and swirled, and then an image began to form . . . a raindrop-speckled water lily from the delta? Suddenly, I was back in the Okavango, exhilaration rushing through me as our little mekoro navigated the submerged hippos. But as quickly as the water lily had come into focus, it vanished again. I squinted to try to bring it back. As I peered into the lights, the object swooning toward me morphed into an old Tibetan pilgrim, sliding forward on his stomach . . . and then a stone face in the Bayon Temple, flickering in and out of being at the whim of the passing shadows.

Just then, the image transformed into the burned woman begging on the streets of Kolkata! I was transported back there in an instant—back to shrieking bedlam and swallowing poverty—and my stomach once again began to churn. *No no no no . . .*

Ben's laugh reeled me back in from the rabbit hole and I gradually realized that I was not in India after all, but in a softly lit café surrounded by my giggly friends who appeared to be conversing with a coconut. I took a deep breath and stabilized myself, then surrendered to the moment and whatever my brain decided to project amid the blossoming colors. As the hallucinations continued, the emotions enmeshed with each experience surged through me like roiling lava. A monkey from Bali brought with it panic . . . an airplane toilet carried a sensual thrill . . . a snow-dusted trail evoked both elation and frustration . . . Some were pleasant, others less so. And I was okay with all of it. I thought, somehow, Amit-ji would be pleased.

When I returned to reality, I discovered that Steve was cradling Ethel and Paul had tied all my dreadlocks to the table behind me. Everyone was starting to sober up and it was getting chilly, so we gathered our belongings and headed back down the mountain. We found Sam tucked up in the boys' room, tired and nauseous but no worse for wear ("You owe me, baaaaabe—I'll acshept a blow job as payment."), and we all cuddled together to wait for morning.

"We lost you for a while up there," said Sara as she lay down beside me. "What were you thinking about?"

"Oh, you know. What a long, strange trip it's been."

She rolled her eyes. "I knew you were going to use that at some point." But even in the dark I could see her grin.

OUR THAI TOURIST visas expired after one month and we had to leave the country to have them reissued, so we went to Singapore for the weekend. We were pretty beaten up from our Full Moon extravaganza—Sara had come down with tonsillitis and I was nursing painful burns on my side. Apparently I'd acquired them during an inopportune encounter with the fiery skipping rope, but I had zero recollection of the event. In any case, we kept our visit to the city-nation mellow, doing little more than window-shopping and drinking bubble tea.

"I can't get over how *clean* this place is," I said, staring incredulously at the immaculate road. "You could, like, have a baby on the sidewalk."

"Remember how clean we thought the Hanoi airport was after India?"

I laughed. "Oh yeah! It's funny, Singapore is the closest we've come to somewhere like home, and yet it seems so foreign to me now. Everything is so modern and organized!"

"Oh god, please don't say the H-word!"

"What H-word? Home?" I paused. "I thought you'd be excited to go home. Well, maybe not *excited*, but . . . you've got your career waiting for you. And you'll move into some cool apartment and settle down."

Sara winced as though I'd slapped her. "That's exactly what I'm *not* looking forward to! A year ago, I had it all planned out: we'd do this trip, I'd get the travel bug out of my system, and then I'd come home and start real life. But I just keep thinking back to what Robert said about how this *is* real life . . ." She trailed off, sighing morosely. "I've never been so confused. It's not that I don't want to be a nurse, because I do. I'm just not ready to stop backpacking yet. They say you're supposed to find yourself while traveling, but I've never felt more lost. And you really scared me the other day—"

"*I* scared you?"

"Yes! Remember when you were talking about how nothing is ever going to impress us again? The job waiting for me, the cool apartment . . . I *used* to want that. Now I'm not so sure. Maybe I just want to be a hippie like you."

I couldn't believe my ears. Perfect Sara was having a *life crisis*? I'd never met anyone with their shit so together, and yet here she was, questioning everything just because I'd said—hey, wait a sec! "Did you just call me a hippie?"

"I mean in the wanderlust way! Although I do recall you quoting the Grateful Dead." She rubbed her temples. "I really don't want to think about this. We've only got a few weeks left. Let's just focus on going out with a bang."

We returned to Thailand and made straight for Koh Tao—an island neighboring Koh Pha Ngan that offers the cheapest diving courses on the continent. Our livers couldn't handle any more abuse and so we opted to focus our energies on obtaining our open water and advanced open water certifications.

One of the requirements for the OW was a written test— mostly regarding safety procedures outlined in the handbook that were easy to memorize. But there was also a mathematical section, necessitating a working knowledge of equations involving the rate of nitrogen expulsion from the body when diving to various depths. And it was here that I floundered like the fish of the same name.

"Look, it's simple algebra," said Sara, as she wrote out the equation for the twelfth time. "Just plug in the numbers from the equation into the formula, and solve for x. No—Sue! You just drew a picture of an octopus eating a shark. That has nothing to do with anything." She peered closer. "And octopuses have eight legs, not ten."

"*Dammit!* I'm never going to get this!" I threw my arms up in frustration. "I can't believe I'm too stupid to dive. I used to think the sky was the limit. Now I realize it's been the sea all along."

"Okay, calm down. You can copy off of my test when the instructor isn't looking. Just promise that when we do go diving, you'll leave the calculations to me."

Thanks to Sara, I passed the exam. Our AOW was far less stressful and included a deep dive, in which the increased nitrogen levels gave us the giggles; a buoyancy-control dive, in which we swam through hoops like circus seals; and a fish-identification dive, in which we were supposed to use names like clownfish and triggerfish but I just called them red fish and blue fish (one fish, two fish). However, by far the most exciting—and terrifying—was the dive that took place at night. The boat set out at ten o'clock, when the water was the color of coal and the sky was sprinkled with stars.

"Everybody stick with your buddies, and keep your flashlights on until I give the cue," said our dive master as we bobbed in the icy waves before our descent. "And remember, no matter what, *don't freak out!*"

"Freak out? Why should I freak out?" I muffled worriedly through my snorkel. "What's down there to freak out about?"

But he had already released the air from his vest and was sinking rapidly, and so I did the same. If the blue abyss had been intimidating, the black abyss was downright *creepy*. The water had become a tangible darkness that stretched in all directions, cold and slimy and potentially sinister. The flashlights were disembodied orbs. Without even bubbles in view, it was almost impossible to tell if we were going down or up or sideways, and my stomach did a monk-style loop-de-loop.

Don't freak out, I ordered myself.

We touched down and began to swim parallel to the ocean floor. We were now able to use our flashlights to investigate our surroundings, and their ghostly rays caught fluorescent flashes of coral splattered on the rocks like exploded paintballs. It was totally disorienting—slices of vibrancy and chaos amid the silent void.

The dive master motioned for us to gather around him in a circle, and he clicked off his flashlight. Panic began to rise in my throat as one by one the flashlights went out until mine was a solitary beam. Everyone looked at me expectantly (or so I assumed—it was hard to tell beneath the masks and mouth-pieces) until I took a deep breath and extinguished my torch. What followed was darkness unlike any I had ever experienced, an all-encompassing blackness in which I not only couldn't see my hand in front of my face, but I also wasn't sure if my eyes were open or closed or even still in their sockets.

Just then, there was a starburst of green sparks. I reeled backward in surprise—what the hell was *that*? But my abrupt movement evoked another surge of the glowing glitter, this time surrounding me like lightning dust. As the color faded, I raised my hand and wiggled my fingers. A cloud of sparkles appeared. Everyone else must've made the same discovery because we all began waving invisible limbs and a galaxy suddenly sprang to life around us—like we'd been transported into space and were witnessing the birth of the universe. Our dive master flapped his arms and legs so forcefully that his entire silhouette was illumin-ated, and I was so awestruck that for one ridiculous second I *almost* thought it was an angel.

"That was *incredible!*" cried Sara when we breached the surface. "What *was* that?"

"They're tiny organisms," explained the dive master. "When you disrupt them, they emit that alien-green bioluminescence."

It was enough to remind me that, while buckets and drugs and two-and-a-half-somes were fun, there were much better reasons to explore the world beyond my front door.

After Koh Tao, time flew by like a peregrine falcon until the next thing we knew we were in Bangkok and it was the final night of our trip.

"So, what should we do?" asked Sara as we sat down to our last Thai curries. "What's our big hurrah?"

We'd spent the day shopping for souvenirs and getting way more Thai massages than necessary—any more relaxed and they'd be soaking us up off the floor with a sponge—but we didn't have anything planned for the evening. I was about to suggest that we do what we'd done every other night (hit the bar and see what happens), when I was interrupted by a plum-shaped woman of about thirty sitting at the table next to ours.

"Excuse me, is that any good?" She motioned to Sara's dinner. "My husband and I just got in today and we have no idea what to order."

Sara and I grinned at each other. Newbies! So eager and clean and pale. I sighed, filled with melancholic nostalgia.

We started talking with them—Amanda and Brody from California—and dinner soon became drinks. Amanda was appalled at the notion of a bucket ("It's fiscal logic," I explained), but Brody was quick to compensate, draining the pails as if he were drinking for them both. Somewhere along the line, we picked up Trevor, an ex-Mormon from Utah who was both wary of a lifestyle he'd been warned against since childhood yet keen to make up for lost time. By midnight, we were *hammered*—skipping and lurching down Khao San Road amid touts that hawked everything under the moon.

"Taxi, taxi, ping-pong show, marijuana, opium, lady, boy, lady boy, taxi!" one guy called out.

"What's a ping-pong show?" asked Trevor.

Sara and I caught eyes and laughed. "It's kind of like a strip show," Sara explained. "Except instead of dancing around a pole, they shoot ping-pong balls out of their, ah, *vajunes*."

"That's *disgusting!*" shrieked Amanda at the exact instant that her husband cried, "We are *so* going!"

She crossed her arms indignantly, and he suggested it be put to a vote. "All in favor of the ping-pong show?"

Brody, me, Sara, Trevor, and the taxi driver all raised our hands. Amanda rolled her eyes and scoffed—but fair was fair and so we piled into the cab. The drive turned out to be much longer than expected, however, and when we stopped it was on a dark street with no other tourists in sight.

"This isn't the backpacker district," said Sara. "Where *are* we?"

We were in front of a squat building, black except for the red light illuminating the entrance. A glowing ember caught my eye—a bouncer stood in the shadows, smoking a cigarette.

"Eight hundred *baht*," he said when we approached the door. "Each."

"Eight hundred? Holy smokes!" cried Trevor. "I got pad thai from a street vendor for thirty."

"Don't worry, it's on me," slurred Brody as he pulled a wad of money out of his shorts.

"Do you remember the exchange rate?" his wife hissed, but he ignored her and handed over a messy stack of bills. The bouncer counted them quickly, then nodded and moved aside so we could pass.

The inside of the club was lit by more red light, which was meant to be sexy but just came off as skeezy. We followed the corridor and went down some stairs, and found ourselves in a small room with plastic tables and a brass pole on a stage. Balloons hung from the ceiling as if left over from a kid's birthday party—no matter what went on here, Rudolph could've probably earned a buck or two. The light was now blue, making us resemble corpses waiting to be autopsied. To make matters even more awkward, we were the only patrons there.

"Drink?" A tired-looking waiter in a wrinkled suit appeared behind us.

"What time does the show start?" asked Brody.

"Show start when you buy drink," said the waiter.

Trevor, Sara, and I exchanged glances. Eight hundred baht and we *still* had to buy alcohol? I opened my mouth to protest but Brody produced yet another handful of crumpled cash. "Buckets for everyone!" he exclaimed, then caught sight of Amanda's murderous scowl. "Uh . . . and a one-ounce cocktail for my better half."

The waiter left to fetch our order and the music started—some American power-ballad from the eighties that had been a joke even then. A woman that could've been anywhere from eighteen to forty took to the stage wearing nothing but glitter. With an underwhelmed expression, she wasted no time in sitting down, spreading her legs, and sticking a ping-pong ball where no ping-pong ball should ever be stuck.

"I wonder how bored she was when she figured out that she could do this," Sara whispered.

"I wonder what happens if she accidentally sucks instead of blows," I whispered back.

There was a pregnant pause and then an almost comical *pop!* The little ball soared through the air before bouncing off the rim of Amanda's glass and rolling off the table and out of sight.

"*Wooooo!*" Brody was on his feet, clapping and whistling as if she'd just scored a touchdown. "That was *incredible!* She almost got it right in your drink, too! Wouldn't *that* have been something special, eh babe?"

With one finger, Amanda pushed the glass as far away from her as possible and glared at Brody in a way that made me question if he was ever going to have sex again. Meanwhile, the performer climbed off the stage and walked over to us holding an empty cup.

"Tip," she said in a voice that made me suspect it was the only English she knew.

"You've *got* to be kidding," said Trevor.

"Tip," she repeated, and because she looked so despondent we all reached into our pockets and procured what we could—except for Brody, that is, who when fishing for money discovered that he'd already spent it all.

A second girl came to the stage. This one was younger (or at least shorter) and without any pretense of apathy. She looked downright miserable, and it was soon apparent why. Her trick was to reach into her *vajune* and—as we drew a collective gasp—slowly pull out a string of razor blades. To demonstrate that they weren't imitations, she held up a folded napkin and carved out little pieces to make a snowflake.

"I was going to decorate our Christmas tree with snowflakes like that!" Amanda recoiled in horror.

"Aw, babe, don't cut up your pussy. You know that's my favorite part of you," said Brody. Sara face-palmed.

This girl also had a cup. "Tip." And after we'd raided our wallets: "More tip."

"*More* tip?" Trevor was incredulous. "Lady, this experience is hurting me way more than it's hurting you."

"More tip!" she insisted, and he sighed guiltily as he handed over the rest of his baht.

While the two girls sat off to the side, a third came onstage in what would turn out to be a very literal triple threat. With the irritated affectation of somebody who wants to check their text messages but can't, she took the same position as the ping-pong champion. However, instead of a ball, she slipped a little dart inside herself. Then, she held a short piece of hollow bamboo up to her crotch, adjusted her pelvis, and—in one fell swoop that defied everything I knew about both physics and vaginas—*launched the dart across the room and popped one of the balloons.*

This time, Brody wasn't the only one cheering. "Wow!" exclaimed Sara with genuine awe. "As a medical professional, allow me to be the first to say, *what the hell?*"

The music changed, and the shorter girl began circling the pole in a manner that was less that of a sultry stripper and more that of a lonely girl at recess who'd lost her tetherball. Meanwhile, the ping-pong champion approached us once again. I thought she was going to request more money but instead she climbed onto the table, inserted another ball, and gestured for Brody to open his mouth. Suddenly, I had a flashback to that moment with Riley and Robyn where I knew what was coming yet for either morbidly curious or mildly diabolical reasons didn't intervene—

Thwunk. It was a hole-in-one.

"Tip."

"*Jesus fucking Christ!*" Amanda leaped to her feet and boxed her husband in the ear. "*What the fuck, Brody? You just caught fucking AIDS!*"

"It's actually very unlikely for AIDS to be contracted orally—" I elbowed Sara in the ribs and she shut up.

"Tip!" echoed the woman with the bamboo tube, and I could tell by her tone that she had no patience for our shenanigans. The girl on the pole burst into silent tears.

But Amanda had her own problems and was not empathetic. "*You whores aren't getting another cent out of us!*" she screamed. "*This place has already cost me an arm and a leg and a motherfucking marriage!*"

"You mad, babe?" Brody muffled with the ping-pong ball still in his mouth.

The woman with the bamboo tube narrowed her eyes and loaded

another dart. This time, though, she aimed her weapon directly at Trevor's face. "Tip!" she spat menacingly. "*Money, falang!*"

"*GAH! NINJA PUSSY BLOW-DART!*" Trevor ducked his head between his knees and shielded himself with his arms. "*Call security!*"

At the mention of "security," the waiter and the bouncer stormed in. There was a lot of rapid Thai as the music scratched and cut and the house lights flooded the room.

"Show over! Everybody out!" the waiter yelled, and we scrambled to leave before somebody lost an eye.

As Amanda ran off sobbing and Brody staggered after her, Trevor, Sara, and I hailed a tuk-tuk.

"I . . . I don't even . . ." Trevor stammered, still in shock. "Okay, I know I'm from Salt Lake, but like—that's not *normal*, right?"

I shook my head. "That was without a doubt one of the most fucked up experiences I've ever had."

"That's good to hear." He took a deep breath. "I think I need to lie down."

And with that, our trip came to an end: a year that began with great white sharks and ended with ninja pussy blow-darts. It hadn't been glamorous, and most of it certainly wasn't comfortable—and thank god, because where would the story be in that?

The journey home from Bangkok was a long one, stretching over forty hours with stopovers in Delhi and Brussels. Sara eventually tumbled into a restless slumber wrought with twitches and whimpers, but I couldn't sleep and instead chased a grape around my fruit cup with a fork. According to the flight map, we were only a couple of hundred miles from Toronto. It was therefore safe to assume that I wasn't going to experience any sort of personal epiphany, after all. But while start-of-the-trip me would've freaked out and written the whole year off as a failure (or at least taken her anger out on the unidentifiable fruit cube that looked like honeydew and tasted like galoshes), end-of-the-trip me felt weirdly unfettered. Actually, looking back, my grand expectations of self-realization seemed almost . . . stupid. I had left home with the idealistic notion of "finding myself"—as if the person I was wasn't adequate and I would find somebody better to be . . . where? Hidden beneath the orange sand on a Namibian dune? Buried beneath a stack of dusty books in a Tibetan monastery? It seemed so ridiculous now. I was still the same neurotic, paranoid person that I'd been a year ago. What I *had* discovered on the road was that being afraid of sharks, monkeys, strenuous exercise, self-reliance, and India didn't make me any less capable than Sara of rising to their challenges. I just did so with a little less grace and a little more complaining. And hey, who's comparing us, anyway?

Just then, Sara woke with a start. Yawning, she asked, "Are we there yet?"

"Almost. Are you okay? You were having a bad dream or something."

"I am *not* looking forward to going home. Like I said, I used to think I had it all figured out. But now . . ." she chewed her fingernail.

"Maybe nobody has it figured out," I offered. "Maybe we all assume we're going to 'get it' when we've achieved this goal or reached that age, but no one actually does, and it's this big inside joke among the old people that there is no secret to life. Just like there are no loop-de-looping monks."

"Um. Wow."

"Impressed with that one?" I grinned.

She patted my arm. "You really need some sleep."

The pilot came over the PA system and announced that we were beginning our descent into Pearson International Airport. As I handed my meal tray to the flight attendant, I said to Sara, "What do you think: reunion tour in twenty years?"

"Done. I wonder if they'll have a Starbucks at Annapurna Base Camp by then."

"Screw Starbucks—I wonder if they'll have escalators!"

And then our plane landed with a bump, and our conversation was cut short as we gathered our belongings and prepared to re-enter real life. Or unreal life. Whatever the case may be.

EPILOGUE
Wherever I Lay My Backpack . . .
DECEMBER: CANADA

Sara's mother: *YOU'RE ALIVE!*

WAS SITTING ON my bed in flannel pajamas with my laptop balanced on my knees. Sara and I had been home for eight days—just long enough for the excitement of seeing my family and the novelty of hot showers to have worn off and been replaced by restless dejection. It was difficult to feel enthusiastic about the present when all I'd done that afternoon was upload five hundred travel photos to Facebook. The snow was slopping against my windowpane in wet clumps, and the pixelated images of pristine beaches and lush jungles intensified my it's-all-over blues.

A dialogue box popped up in the corner of my screen. *Hi lady!* It was Paul.

What's up? I responded. *Where are you now?*

In Sydney w Ben Steve and Sam. They got yr-long work visas. Ben had his tattoo gun shipped over and is settin up shop. There was a pause in which I could see him typing, then deleting, then re-typing, then stopping.

What happened? I wrote.

Well . . . we were partying hard in memory of Full Moon. And I think karma for that roofie finally caught up with me because I dont remember anything except wakin up w a really weird pain in my arse.

There was another pause, and then a notification that I'd been tagged in a picture. I clicked to investigate—then jumped backward in surprise, whacking the back of my head on the wall behind me.

Staring me square in the face was Paul's ass, hairy and Irish and sporting a crusty tattoo of—Jesus, what *was* that? It looked sort of like a happy face, except oddly furry. As I leaned forward,

I noticed a name scrawled below in loopy calligraphy, and nearly fell off the bed in a fit of hysterics.

It was Ethel the coconut.

ACKNOWLEDGMENTS

Many thanks to Rasia Virani for her incredible manuscript edits, unwavering project devotion, and wonderful teatime conversation; Sara for every backpacking (mis)adventure; my parents, who will be receiving a censored version of this book; Babcia and Nana for ensuring I wasn't literally a starving artist; Jack for his support throughout the process; Aimee and Shira for two decades of listening to my stories; Taryn and Colin at Brindle & Glass; and everybody I met while out and about in 2010.

S. BEDFORD is an indie backpacker who has accidentally locked herself in the bathroom in over fifty countries. She calls Toronto, Canada, home base, and *It's Only the Himalayas* is her first book.